Rainbow English Programme for Primary Schools

RAINBOW
ENGLISH PROGRAMME
6
SIXTH CLASS BOOK

Flying High!

Portfolio Book

CJ Fallon
ESTABLISHED 1895

MERIEL McCORD   DEIRDRE MULLIGAN

KEVIN BARRY   ANDRÉE MULVIHILL

STAGE 4
BOOK 2

Published by

CJ Fallon

Ground Floor – Block B

Liffey Valley Office Campus

Dublin 22

ISBN: 978-0-7144-2723-2

First Edition June 2019

This Reprint April 2021

Printed in Ireland by

W&G Baird Limited

Caulside Drive

Antrim BT41 2RS

Introduction

This ground-breaking **Portfolio Book** accompanies the core book *Flying High!* It reinforces the comprehension, vocabulary, word study/phonics, grammar and punctuation covered in the core book. A unique feature of the Portfolio Book is that it covers all the **writing genres**. All writing activities/genres are modelled in the dedicated **online writing activities** section. The Portfolio Book is a clear record of the student's work for the year.

The Writing Genres

1. **Recount writing:** tells about the events in the order in which they happened. You can recount stories or events from storybooks, diaries, newspaper articles, history books and eyewitness accounts.

2. **Report writing:** describes and gives clear information about objects, places, animals or people. You can make reports on newspaper articles, fiction or non-fiction books, games, meetings, races, a robbery, accidents, school sports day, parades and concerts.

3. **Explanatory writing:** explains how or why things occur. Examples of explanatory writing can be found in science books, on the internet, non-fiction books, SESE books or in encyclopedias.

4. **Narrative writing:** entertains and engages the reader in an imaginative experience. It includes the character(s), the setting and the event(s) leading to a problem and a solution to the same problem. Examples of narrative writing can be found in storybooks, novels, fairy tales, fables, myths, legends, plays and poems.

5. **Persuasive writing:** is used to persuade others by involving argument and debate. Persuasive writing should have an introduction to the topic, a middle section discussing the topic in more depth and must finish with a final conclusion. Examples of persuasive writing are in debates, book and film reviews and advertisements.

6. **Writing to socialise:** is used to maintain or enhance relationships. It can be formal or informal, depending on the relationship between the writer and the audience, e.g. postcards, letters, emails, texts, notes of apology, invitations and messages.

7. **Procedural writing:** contains a set of step-by-step instructions for doing something, e.g. a recipe or list of instructions for operating a machine, etc. Examples of procedural writing can be found in recipe and cookery books, assembly kits, rules for games, science books and maps.

8. **Free writing:** is used when you decide to use any genre of writing on any subject.

Note: Pupils are asked to research using the library or the internet. This should be done under the supervision of a teacher, parent or guardian at all times.

Scoil Mhuire na Trócaire
Buttevant Co Cork
Tel: 022-23506
Email@ buttevantprimaryschool@gmail.com

Contents

1 What Not to Do If You Turn Invisible

A A Little Light Thinking

1. What age is Ethel? _____

2. Where was Ethel when she turned invisible?_____

3. How does Lady react when Ethel starts to pet her?

   _____

4. What is Gram's remedy for calming nerves?

   _____

5. Why did Ethel go on the sunbed?_____

6. For how long was Ethel asleep on the sunbed? _____

7. Where was Gram attending the meeting? _____

8. Who is the author of the story?_____

B Deeper Thinking

1. Why do you think Lady looked *scared and confused*? _____

   _____

2. What kind of a meeting do you think Gram was attending?_____

   _____

3. Why didn't Ethel tell her friend Kirsten about turning invisible?_____

   _____

4. What is the meaning of the word *preposterous*? _____

   _____

5. In what way did Gram miss the point when Ethel said that she had become invisible?

   _____

   _____

6. Why do you think Gram's tone of voice changed from sympathetic to stern?

   _____

   _____

CHALLENGE

Being invisible would be a great advantage in life.
Give two reasons why you agree or disagree with this statement.

(a) _____

(b) _____

C Vocabulary Work: Wordsearch

Ring the words in the wordsearch.

a	u	a	u	t	o	m	a	t	i	c	a	l	l	y
d	r	r	h	y	s	t	e	r	i	c	a	l	i	f
e	l	x	a	a	i	a	f	t	y	c	o	s	m	l
r	e	l	a	n	e	o	r	l	i	e	i	t	a	m
a	r	w	a	d	i	o	e	t	f	n	s	e	g	r
e	z	e	n	c	r	t	e	m	y	a	s	r	i	e
p	z	w	s	r	i	h	h	b	k	d	e	i	n	v
p	e	e	i	n	t	t	y	m	k	n	r	c	a	i
a	a	m	i	a	r	y	a	h	i	u	p	a	r	t
s	y	f	p	p	j	a	a	m	f	m	x	l	y	c
i	e	m	m	y	z	n	b	w	o	f	e	k	x	e
d	y	t	i	n	v	i	s	i	b	l	e	u	l	f
s	s	i	t	c	e	f	f	e	y	u	u	v	m	f
e	p	r	e	s	u	m	a	b	l	y	e	a	z	e
z	v	e	x	p	r	e	s	s	i	o	n	s	v	z

invisible →
mundane ↑
mirror ↗
automatically →
expressions →
definitely ↗
presumably →
effective ↑
imaginary ↓
disappeared ↑
hysterical →
sympathetic ↗

D Grammar: Singular and Plural

To form the plural of nouns ending in a consonant + y, change the y to i and add **es**, e.g. fly → fl**ies** / body → bod**ies** / country → countr**ies** / county → count**ies**.
To form the plural of nouns ending in a vowel + y, just add **s**, e.g. boy → boy**s** / journey → journey**s** / railway → railway**s** / jersey → jersey**s**.

Write the correct plural form of each singular noun below.

(a) industry: _____   (b) property: _____   (c) storey: _____

(d) story: _____   (e) balcony: _____   (f) chimney: _____

(g) gallery: _____   (h) attorney: _____   (i) visibility: _____

(j) disability: _____   (k) hurley: _____   (l) opportunity: _____

(m) array: _____   (n) volley: _____   (o) biography: _____

(p) decay: _____   (q) agency: _____   (r) summary: _____

(s) display: _____   (t) city: _____   (u) capacity: _____

(v) boy: _____   (w) journey: _____   (x) canary: _____

(y) category: _____   (z) daisy: _____

1 What Not to Do If You Turn Invisible

E **Grammar: Capital Letters and Full Stops**

> Sentences start with a capital letter and end with a full stop.
> Capital letters are also used for: (a) the names of people, places and languages, (b) the titles of books, newspapers, plays and films, (c) the pronoun I, (d) special days, e.g. St Patrick's Day.

Rewrite the following sentences using capital letters and full stops.

1. always use a capital letter when starting a sentence

   _____

2. when writing my name and surname, i start with a capital letter

   _____

3. the initial letters of my address are also written with capital letters

   _____

4. my address is _____, _____, _____

5. i live in Ireland and i speak english and irish

   _____

6. ireland's patron saint is celebrated on _____ _____ _____,

   which falls on _____ 17th every year

7. parades are held on this national holiday to celebrate irish culture

   _____

8. my favourite book is _____ and

   my favourite film is _____

9. the person whom i most admire is _____

10. the *harry potter* books were written by jk rowling

    _____

F **Extension Ideas**

Use the library or internet to help you with the following exercise.

The idea of a character or an object becoming invisible is a common plot device in fantasy fiction. Write about another story you have read or a film you have watched about invisibility.

1. Title of story/film: _____

2. Who/what became invisible? _____

3. How did the character/object become invisible? _____

   _____

4. How did the character/object behave while invisible? _____

   _____

5. Could the character/object return to being visible? _____

6. If so, how could this happen? _____

   _____

G Writing Genre: Recount Writing

You are Ethel. Plan and write the story of the day you turned invisible.
Complete the template below.

Title: **The Day I Became Invisible**

When did it happen? _____

Who is the story about? _____

What happened? _____

Where did it happen? _____

Why did it happen? _____

Event 1: First, _____

Event 2: Next, _____

Event 3: After that, _____

Event 4: Finally, _____

Afterwards, how did you feel? _____

Now, recount your story.

Title: **The Day I Became Invisible**

_____
_____
_____
_____
_____
_____
_____

_____
_____
_____
_____
_____
_____
_____
_____
_____
_____
_____
_____
_____
_____
_____
_____
_____
_____
_____
_____
_____
_____
_____

H Self Reflection

I was good at: _____

I need to do more work on: _____ Date: _____

A A Little Light Thinking

1. Why was Stephanie surprised when the phone rang?

   _____

2. Why did Stephanie like shouting?

   _____

3. How did the man get into the house?

   _____

4. What did the man ask Stephanie to give him as he sneered?

   _____

5. How did the man say he came to know about Skulduggery Pleasant?

   _____

6. Describe how the man reacted when he was covered in flames.

   _____

B Deeper Thinking

1. How do you know that the owner of the house had died recently?

   _____

2. Why do you think the man wanted to get into the house?

   _____

   _____

3. What evidence in the story tells us that Stephanie was a brave girl?

   _____

   _____

4. Why do you think Skulduggery Pleasant arrived at the house?

   _____

5. Give two examples of how the man wasn't injured easily.

   (a) _____

   (b) _____

6. What do you think Stephanie did after the man left the house?

   _____

   _____

CHALLENGE

Research who Gordon Edgley was and why Stephanie was alone in his house that night.

_____

_____

C Vocabulary Work: Crossword

Complete the crossword using the clues below.

ACROSS
2. Crashed into/banged against
3. Average/normal
4. Thumping/beating strongly
6. Disobediently
8. An abundance of money

DOWN
1. Wailed/moaned
2. Twisting/distorting
5. Became aware of/noticed
7. Anger/rage
9. Panic

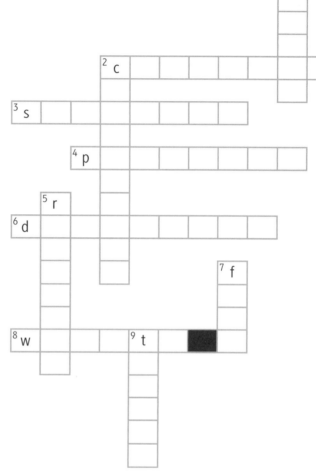

D Working with Sounds: Silent Letters

Remember: Some words contain **silent letters** that we don't sound out, e.g. listen, knew, etc.

Read the words in the word box and then write them under the correct headings in the grid below.

doubt	wrong	sword	hedge	mortgage	salmon
half	design	sign	answer	debt	knee
dawn	thumb	could	chalk	grudge	know
handkerchief	Wednesday	write	handsome	campaign	plumber
knuckle	pledge	lamb	knock	reign	foreign
talk	fasten	dumb	walk	glisten	bustle
castle	knife	gnaw	wrist	listen	knot

Silent b	Silent d	Silent g	Silent k	Silent l	Silent t	Silent w

E Grammar: Punctuation Marks

Always put a **full stop**, a **question mark** or an **exclamation mark** at the end of a sentence.
A **question mark** /?/ is used after a question is asked, e.g. Where is Stephanie?
An **exclamation mark** /!/ is used to show surprise, joy or anger. It is like writing in a loud voice, e.g. 'Stop shouting!' the teacher said loudly.
A **full stop** /./ is used at the end of a sentence.

Rewrite the following using capital letters and missing punctuation marks.

1. 'hello' stephanie repeated when she heard the knock

   _____

2. 'who is this' the man asked from outside the house

   _____

3. 'i'm sorry' stephanie said, 'who are you looking for'

   _____

4. 'who is this' responded the voice, more irritably this time

   _____

5. 'if you are looking for gordon edgley,' stephanie said, i'm afraid that he's –'

   _____

6. 'i know edgley's dead, snapped the man 'who are you'

   _____

7. stephanie hesitated 'why do you want to know' she asked

   _____

8. 'what are you doing in that house why are you in that house'

   _____

9. 'you don't talk to me like that' the man hissed

   _____

10. 'open up' came the man's voice between the pounding

   _____

F Extension Ideas

Use the library or internet to help you with the following exercise.
Skulduggery Pleasant **is the first book in a series of books.**

1. **Who wrote the series?** _____

2. **Name three other books in the series.**

   (a) _____

   (b) _____

   (c) _____

3. **What is the main background story behind the series?**

   _____

   _____

G Writing Genre: Recount Writing

Pretend that you are Stephanie. Plan and write the story of the day you met Skulduggery Pleasant for the first time. Complete the template below.

Title: **The Day I Met Skulduggery Pleasant for the First Time**

Setting: _____

When did it happen? _____

Who is the story about? _____

Where did it happen? _____

What were they doing? _____

Why did it happen? _____

Event 1: First, _____

Event 2: Next, _____

Event 3: After that, _____

Event 4: Finally, _____

Afterwards, how did you feel? _____

Now, recount your story.

Title: **The Day I Met Skulduggery Pleasant for the First Time**

_____

_____

_____

_____

_____

_____

_____

_____
_____
_____
_____
_____
_____
_____
_____
_____
_____
_____
_____
_____
_____
_____
_____
_____
_____
_____
_____
_____
_____
_____
_____
_____
_____

H **Self Reflection**

I was good at: _____

I need to do more work on: _____ Date: _____

A **A Little Light Thinking**

1. What genre of novel is the most popular with readers?

   _____

2. When did the fictional *Sherlock Holmes* first appear in a short novel?

   _____

3. Who is the author of the *Sherlock Holmes* detective stories?

   _____

4. What were the names of the four *Sherlock Holmes* novels?

   (a) _____ (b) _____

   (c) _____ (d) _____

5. Where are most of the *Sherlock Holmes* novels set? _____

6. How did Sherlock Holmes describe Professor James Moriarty?

   _____

7. Why did Conan Doyle have to revive Sherlock Holmes after killing him off?

   _____

8. From what country is the private investigator Hercule Poirot? _____

B **Deeper Thinking**

1. How do you think detectives can use fingerprints to solve crimes?

   _____

   _____

2. Why do you think detective novels is the most popular genre of novel?

   _____

   _____

3. What personality traits did Sherlock Holmes have that enabled him to be good at his job?

   _____

   _____

4. What do you think Sherlock Holmes meant by the phrase: *Elementary, my dear Watson*?

   _____

   _____

5. Why do you think detective stories are sometimes called *Whodunit* stories?

   _____

   _____

What is your favourite book genre? Explain.

_____

_____

C Vocabulary Work: Work Like a Detective

Read the clues to solve the names and ages of each character below.

_____ _____ _____ _____ _____

(Names)

_____ _____ _____ _____ _____

(Ages)

1. The woman with the cats is 30 years old.
2. Harry is 55 years old.
3. Edward is to the left of Bob.
4. Janet is next to the oldest man.
5. The tallest man is 40 years old.
6. The youngest woman is 25 years old.
7. Sally likes music.
8. The short man is 35 years old.

D Comprehension Work: Cloze Procedure

Use the words in the word box to complete the story below.

tidy	famous	sold	years	written
time	featuring	solve	short	clever
clues	glasses	moustache	nose	eyes
detective	problems	talk	working	shape

Hercule Poirot

Agatha Christie was a _____ crime novelist who wrote between the _____ 1920 and 1975. She's listed in the *Guinness Book of Records* as the best-selling novelist of all _____. Her novels have _____ about 2 billion copies worldwide. Her novel *Murder on the Orient Express*, _____ the Belgian detective Hercule Poirot, was _____ in 1934. Hercule Poirot is described as a _____ man with a head exactly the _____ of an egg. He has an upward curling _____, which looks very stiff and military. He has a pink-tipped _____ and his clothes are always incredibly neat and _____. He wears *pince-nez* reading _____ and his green _____ shine like a cat's when he is struck by a _____ idea. The poor man suffers badly from stomach _____ and seasickness.

In the early books, Poirot is a clue-based and logical _____. In his own words, he uses his little grey cells as well as order and method to _____ crimes. However, in later books, Poirot relies more on _____ out the psychology of the murderer and getting people to _____ and so give away _____ that he uses to solve the most complex crimes.

E Grammar: Commas

A comma /,/ is used:

(a) to show a sequence of actions, e.g. I opened the door, stepped outside and shut the door behind me.

(b) to separate items in any type of list, e.g. There were sleeping bags, pans, warm clothing and boots in the tent.

(c) to introduce a present participle verb /-ing/ in a sentence, e.g. Wagging its tail, my dog ran up to me.

(d) to introduce or interrupt direct quotations, e.g. She sighed, 'You'll be late again.' / 'I don't care,' he replied.

(e) after a word such as *however*, *furthermore* or *therefore* used at the beginning of a sentence, e.g. However, she was unable to open the door.

Rewrite the following sentences inserting commas in the correct places.

1. Conan Doyle's four novels were *A Study in Scarlet The Sign of the Four The Hound of the Baskervilles* and *The Valley of Fear*.

   _____

2. 'I know who committed the crime' said Miss Marple.

   _____

3. Dr Watson is a gentle simple plodding and intelligent type of person.

   _____

4. Miss Marple was a prim bird-like elderly lady who lived in the village St Mary Mead.

   _____

5. Writing for younger readers Derek Landy has become a very popular author.

   _____

6. However the detective genre is still hugely popular among readers.

   _____

7. California Alaska Utah and Alabama are all states in America.

   _____

8. 'I like to read detective novels' stated the boy.

   _____

F Extension Ideas

Use the library or internet to help you with the following exercise.

1. **Who inspired the character of Sherlock Holmes?**

   _____

2. **Where in London is the Sherlock Holmes Museum?**

   _____

3. **Describe the furnishings of the Sherlock Holmes Museum.**

   _____

4. **Why did Conan Doyle choose Dr Watson to narrate the Sherlock Holmes stories?**

   _____

G **Writing Genre: Report Writing**

Research, plan and write a report on one of the following:
(a) famous musicians, (b) famous artists, (c) famous inventors, or (d) famous actors.
Complete the template below.

Title: **Famous** _____

What does he/she do? _____

Who are they? _____

When does this take place? _____

Description (personal details): _____

What significant things is he/she famous for? _____

Summarising comment: _____

Now, write your report.

Title: **Famous** _____

_____

_____

_____

_____

_____

_____

_____

_____

_____

_____

_____

_____

_____

_____

_____

_____

_____

_____

_____

_____

_____

_____

_____

_____

_____

_____

_____

_____

_____

_____

_____

_____

_____

_____

_____

_____

H Self Reflection

I was good at: _____

I need to do more work on: _____ Date: _____

The Girl in the White Nightdress 4

A A Little Light Thinking

1. What did Anna give Evie to wear? _____

2. Describe what happened after the clock struck 12.

_____

3. Who or what was staring back at Evie from the window?

_____

4. What did Evie do when the girl in the window beckoned to her?

_____

5. Describe the middle-aged woman who opened the door of Anna's bedroom.

_____

6. Why did Evie pinch herself as she walked down the corridor?

_____

7. What wafted up the stairs? _____

8. Where did the man say they were waiting for her? _____

B Deeper Thinking

1. To what past era do you think Evie travelled back?

_____

2. If you had the opportunity, to what past era would you like to travel? Explain.

_____

_____

3. What sentence tells us that Evie was terrified when she saw the girl at the window?

_____

_____

4. What sentence marks the transition from the present to the past?

_____

_____

5. How did the décor (style) of the house change when Evie travelled back in time?

_____

_____

CHALLENGE

List three jobs done by a scullery maid during the Victorian era.

(a) _____

(b) _____

(c) _____

C Vocabulary Work: Synonyms – Thesaurus Work

Synonyms are words that are similar, or close to similar, in meaning, e.g. enormous → huge.

Write two synonyms for the underlined word in each sentence.

1. The ghosts in the chimney <u>howled</u> even louder. (a) _____ (b) _____
2. The water stopped <u>gurgling</u> in the pipes. (a) _____ (b) _____
3. My teeth were chattering and I <u>shivered</u>. (a) _____ (b) _____
4. The girl had a <u>desperate</u> look in her eyes. (a) _____ (b) _____
5. I saw my <u>reflection</u> in the window. (a) _____ (b) _____
6. Evie thought that she was <u>hallucinating</u>. (a) _____ (b) _____
7. The hand <u>beckoned</u> to me to move. (a) _____ (b) _____
8. The sugar had <u>dissolved</u> in the mixture. (a) _____ (b) _____
9. The door was <u>elaborately</u> panelled. (a) _____ (b) _____
10. The floor gleamed in the <u>flickering</u> lamplight. (a) _____ (b) _____
11. In a fog of <u>confusion</u>, she gripped the rail. (a) _____ (b) _____
12. Delicious food smells <u>wafted</u> up the stairs. (a) _____ (b) _____

D Grammar: Common Nouns and Proper Nouns

A **common noun** is the name of any person, place, animal or thing, e.g. boy, shop, dog, table. A **proper noun** is the name of a **particular** person, place, animal or brand, e.g. Sofia, Cork, Frankie the dog, Lego. Proper nouns must always start with a capital letter.

1. **In table 1, write a proper noun (a specific name) next to each of the common nouns.**
2. **In table 2, write a common noun next to each of the proper nouns.**

Table 1		Table 2	
Common Noun	**Proper Noun**	**Common Noun**	**Proper Noun**
(a) boy			(a) Paris
(b) girl			(b) Rex
(c) town			(c) Tabby
(d) doctor			(d) Loch Allen
(e) teacher			(e) Mount Everest
(f) lake			(f) John
(g) county			(g) Sarah
(h) country			(h) January
(i) weekday			(i) France
(j) month			(j) Clare
(k) mountain			(k) Achill
(l) river			(l) Sahara
(m) island			(m) Atlantic

E Working with Sounds: The /f/ Sound Spelled with ph

The /f/ sound is spelled using the letters **ph** in words of Greek origin, e.g. **ph**otogra**ph**, s**ph**ere.

1. Write the correct **ph** word from the word box in each sentence.

sphere	photograph	paragraph	apostrophe	pharmacy
alphabet	elephant	dolphin	phobia	emphasis
trophy	typhoon	physical	catastrophe	phonics

(a) A football is an example of this 3-D shape: _____.

(b) An object awarded as a prize for a victory or success is a _____.

(c) A distinct section in a piece of writing is called a _____.

(d) This can mean stress given to a word to indicate its importance: _____.

(e) A picture made using light and a camera is called a _____.

(f) A shop where a chemist or pharmacist works is called a _____.

(g) A punctuation mark used to show ownership is called an _____.

(h) A very large, plant-eating mammal with a trunk is called an _____.

(i) A tropical storm in the region of the western Pacific Ocean is called a _____.

(j) Another word for a major disaster is a _____.

(k) An irrational fear of something is called a _____.

(l) This small sea mammal is loved by most people: _____.

(m) The method of teaching reading through letter sounds is called _____.

(n) A, B, C, D, E are all letters of the _____.

(o) P.E. is an abbreviation for the school subject _____ education.

2. Ring the correctly spelled word on each line.

(a)	fotograf	photograf	fotograph	photograph	photagraph
(b)	pharmacist	farmacist	pharmicist	pharrmacist	pharmasist
(c)	apostrofe	apostrophe	appostrophe	aprosstrophe	apostroffie
(d)	paragraph	paragraf	parragraph	pragraph	piragrgh
(e)	alfabet	alphabeth	alphabet	alfabeth	allphabet
(f)	tifoon	tyfoon	typoon	tyffoon	typhoon
(g)	emphasis	emfasis	imphasis	enphasis	emphassis
(h)	trofy	trofie	trophy	trophey	trofey

F Extension Ideas

Use the library or internet to help you find out more information about clothing during the Victorian era.

1. Wealthy ladies wore _____

_____

2. Wealthy gentlemen wore _____

_____

3. Female servants wore _____

_____

G **Writing Genre: Report Writing**

Research, plan and write a report on Hallowe'en. Complete the template below.

Title: **Hallowe'en**

Classification: What is Hallowe'en? _____

When did the tradition of Hallowe'en begin? _____

Where is Hallowe'en celebrated? _____

How is Hallowe'en celebrated? _____

_____

Summarising comment: _____

_____

Now, write your report.

Title: **Hallowe'en**

_____

_____

_____

_____

_____

_____

_____

_____

_____

_____

_____

_____

_____
_____
_____
_____
_____
_____
_____
_____
_____
_____
_____
_____
_____
_____
_____
_____
_____
_____
_____
_____
_____
_____
_____
_____

H **Self Reflection**

I was good at: _____

I need to do more work on: _____ Date: _____

5 There to Here

A A Little Light Thinking

1. Where in Ireland do Tanza and her family live? _____

2. What problem has Tanza's mother with cooking at the centre?

   _____

3. Name some Irish foods that Tanza and her family get to eat at the centre.

   _____

4. Why does Tanza like to go to the Phoenix Park after school?

   _____

5. Why did Benjamin warn Tanza to stay away from the Phoenix Park?

   _____

6. How do you know that Tanza doesn't speak fluent English?

   _____

7. Who is the boy hiding in the bushes? _____

8. What sentences tell us that Benjamin is finding it difficult to be head of the family?

   _____

B Deeper Thinking

1. What aspect of life at the centre does Tanza's mother find the most difficult?

   _____

   _____

2. Why do you think Tanza and her family are living at the centre?

   _____

   _____

3. What aspects of school life does Tanza find difficult?

   _____

   _____

4. Why do you think that Benjamin is finding the responsibility of being head of the family
   very difficult? _____

   _____

5. Why do you think Benjamin has turned bossy?

   _____

   _____

6. What sentence in the story suggests that girls in Tanza's home country do not
   have the same freedom with education and jobs that they have in Ireland?

   _____

   _____

CHALLENGE

Write the names of six buildings situated in the Phoenix Park.

(a) _____   (b) _____

(c) _____   (d) _____

(e) _____   (f) _____

C **Vocabulary Work: Dictionary Meanings**

Write the dictionary meanings of the following words.

(a) permission: _____

(b) indignation: _____

(c) foreign: _____

(d) queue: _____

(e) traditional: _____

(f) shadow: _____

(g) recognise: _____

(h) flicker: _____

(i) centre: _____

(j) avenue: _____

(k) enclosed: _____

(l) fluttering: _____

D **Working with Sounds: The Consonant Digraph /ch/**

The consonant digraph /ch/ has **three** different sounds. The most common sounds are: (a) /ch/ as in **ch**ildren, (b) /sh/ as in **ch**ef and, (c) /k/ as in ar**ch**itect and other words of Greek origin.

1. **Complete the following sentences using the /ch/ words from the word box.**

Chaos	chemist	chimney	echo	moustache	architect
mechanic	brochure	orchid	chef	monarch	parachute

(a) An _____ is an ornamental plant with a delicate flower.

(b) A _____ is a book or magazine containing pictures and information about a product or service.

(c) An _____ is a sound or sounds caused by the reflection of sound waves from a surface back to the listener.

(d) A person who designs buildings is called an _____.

(e) A _____ is a strip of hair left to grow above the upper lip.

(f) A _____ is a canopy that allows you to descend slowly from an aircraft.

(g) A person who works as a professional cook is called a _____.

(h) _____ means complete disorder and confusion.

(i) A _____ is a pipe that conducts smoke up from a fire.

(j) A king or queen is also called a _____.

(k) A person who repairs engines and other machinery is called a _____.

(l) Another name for a pharmacist is a _____.

2. **The seven words in the word box above in which /ch/ has a /k/ sound are:**

(a) _____ (b) _____ (c) _____ (d) _____

(e) _____ (f) _____ (g) _____

3. **The four words in the word box above in which /ch/ has an /sh/ sound are:**

(a) _____ (b) _____ (c) _____ (d) _____

E **Grammar: Collective Nouns**

A **collective noun** is used to represent a group of (a) people, e.g. a **company** of actors, (b) animals, e.g. a **clowder** of cats, or (c) things, e.g. a **bale** of briquettes.

Complete the following using the correct collective noun from the word box.

plague	quiver	herd	set	litter	string	army
flock	deck	pair	gaggle	school	forest	swarm
wad	bouquet	coven	team	galaxy	pack	range
	choir	band	flight	chest	field	

(a) a _____ of bees

(b) a _____ of drawers

(c) a _____ of fish

(d) a _____ of pigs

(e) a _____ of buffalo

(f) a _____ of arrows

(g) an _____ of soldiers

(h) a _____ of players

(i) a _____ of wolves

(j) a _____ of china

(k) a _____ of sheep

(l) a _____ of runners

(m) a _____ of horses

(n) a _____ of locusts

(o) a _____ of witches

(p) a _____ of musicians

(q) a _____ of geese

(r) a _____ of birds

(s) a _____ of shoes

(t) a _____ of singers

(u) a _____ of cards

(v) a _____ of trees

(w) a _____ of stars

(x) a _____ of mountains

(y) a _____ of notes

(z) a _____ of flowers

F **Extension Ideas**

Use the library or internet to help you with the following exercise.

1. Find out more information and write an explanatory note on the International Protection Act 2015.

   _____

   _____

2. What is the meaning of the term *direct provision*?

   _____

   _____

3. List the names of four direct provision centres in Ireland past or present.

   (a) _____

   (b) _____

   (c) _____

   (d) _____

G **Writing Genre: Explanation Writing**

Research, plan and write an explanation for: *How a Refugee Can Apply for Asylum in Ireland.* Complete the template below.

Title: **How a Refugee Can Apply for Asylum in Ireland**

Definition: What is a refugee? _____

_____

What countries are affected? _____

_____

How does it work? _____

_____

When and where it works or is applied: _____

_____

Interesting comments: _____

_____

Special features: _____

_____

Evaluation: _____

_____

Now, write your explanation.

Title: **How a Refugee Can Apply for Asylum in Ireland**

_____

_____

_____

_____

_____

_____

_____

_____

_____

_____

_____

_____

_____

_____

_____

_____

_____

_____

_____

_____

_____

_____

_____

_____

_____

_____

_____

_____

_____

_____

H **Self Reflection**

I was good at: _____

I need to do more work on: _____ Date: _____

A **A Little Light Thinking**

1. What animals were hunted in the Phoenix Park?

   (a) _____ (b) _____

2. What is the name of the main road in the Phoenix Park? _____

3. What is stored in most of the rooms at Áras an Uachtaráin?

   _____

4. Name three US presidents who have stayed at Áras an Uachtaráin.

   (a) _____ (b) _____

   (c) _____

5. How much did it cost to refurbish Farmleigh House? _____

6. How many animals, in total, were donated by London Zoo to Dublin Zoo? _____

7. Explain why the Magazine Fort was built in a star shape.

   _____

8. How was Ashtown Castle rediscovered?

   _____

B **Deeper Thinking**

1. Why do you think that the Phoenix Park is totally enclosed?

   _____
   _____

2. Why do you think we need an official state guesthouse in Ireland?

   _____
   _____

3. Why do you think the British army chose the Phoenix Park as the location
   for their main magazine fort in Ireland? _____

   _____

4. Why do you think the tunnel running under the Phoenix Park was closed?

   _____

5. Write three reasons why you think zoos were opened around the world.

   (a) _____

   (b) _____

   (c) _____

6. Why do you think the walls of the Magazine Fort were built 1.5 metres thick?

   _____

CHALLENGE

In your opinion, the phoenix rising from the ashes is a symbol for what?

_____
_____

C **Vocabulary Work: What Does It Mean?**

Complete the following sentences to show the meaning of the underlined word or phrase.

1. The <u>residence</u> _____

2. The walls <u>enclosed</u> _____

3. <u>Áras an Uachtaráin</u> _____

4. The <u>Magazine Fort</u> was used for _____

5. The <u>train tunnel</u> _____

6. The <u>Papal Cross</u> _____

7. London Zoo <u>donated</u> _____

8. The <u>thatched</u> roof _____

9. The Phoenix <u>Monument</u> _____

10. The <u>ambassador</u> _____

D **Comprehension Work: Cloze Procedure**

Use the words in the word box to complete the story below.

urban	fallow	demolished	year	fourth
Dublin	Ireland	Farmleigh	stately	tunnel
Ashtown	walking	facilities	hunted	rediscovered
Phoenix	century	president	Heuston	roamed

The Phoenix Park

The _____ Park is one of the largest _____ parks in the world. It contains a number of _____ homes, including the official residence of our _____. Other stately residences in the Phoenix Park are the Deerfield Residence and _____ House.

The park is home to a large herd of _____ deer. Deer have _____ freely there since the 17th _____, when they were _____ for sport.

The park is open to the public seven days a week, all _____ round. Contained within the park are a number of sports _____ and cycling and _____ routes. The park is also home to _____ Zoo, which is said to be the _____ oldest zoo in the world.

Adjoining the Visitor Centre is the fully restored _____ Castle, a medieval tower house dating back to the 1430s. This building was _____ when Ashtown Lodge was being _____ in 1978.

A train tunnel connecting _____ Station and Connolly Station runs below the park. This _____ is approximately 140 years old and there are plans to open it to the public in the near future.

The park is home to the Phoenix Park Cricket Club, the oldest cricket club in _____, founded in 1830.

E **Grammar: Gender of Nouns**

1. **Fill in the blanks with the opposite masculine or feminine nouns.**

(a) hero: _____   (b) countess: _____   (c) bride: _____

(d) prince: _____   (e) drake: _____   (f) bull: _____

(g) headmaster: _____   (h) daughter: _____   (i) queen: _____

(j) waitress: _____   (k) duke: _____   (l) actor: _____

(m) mother: _____   (n) sister: _____   (o) tiger: _____

(p) host: _____   (q) mare: _____   (r) ram: _____

(s) giantess: _____   (t) niece: _____   (u) aunt: _____

2. **Write the words from the word box in the correct column in the grid below.**

brother	monument	niece	child	tunnel	pupil	daughter	lake
king	television	plate	parent	bird	sister	mother	uncle
teacher	grandfather	cousin	person	ladder	roof	aunt	boy
table	telephone	ram	baby	vixen	wife	bull	princess
friend	bachelor	fish	stallion	gate	lord	lady	lioness

Masculine	Feminine	Common	Neuter

F **Extension Ideas**

Use the library or internet to help you with the following exercise.

1. **Name four sports that take place at the Phoenix Park.**

(a) _____   (b) _____

(c) _____   (d) _____

2. **Name four famous bands that played in concert at the Phoenix Park.**

(a) _____   (b) _____

(c) _____   (d) _____

3. **Name four presidents of Ireland who have lived at Áras an Uachtaráin.**

(a) _____

(b) _____

(c) _____

(d) _____

G Writing Genre: Explanation Writing

Many animals throughout the world are endangered – they are in danger of becoming extinct. This is due to changing environments and because they are being hunted by predators. Plan and write an explanation for how Dublin Zoo helps conserve endangered animals. Complete the template below.

Title: **How Dublin Zoo Helps Conserve Endangered Animals**

Definition: What is conservation? _____

How does it happen? _____

Where does it happen? _____

When does it happen? _____

Why does it happen? _____

Endangered animals that have been bred successfully at Dublin Zoo:

_____

Special features: Why is it important to protect endangered animals?

_____

_____

Now, write your explanation.

Title: **How Dublin Zoo Helps Conserve Endangered Animals**

_____

_____

_____

_____

_____

_____

_____

_____

I was good at: _____

I need to do more work on: _____ Date: _____

7 How to Recognise a Witch

Ⓐ A Little Light Thinking

1. What does the story tell us that a real witch has instead of fingernails?

   _____

2. How does a real witch disguise her baldness?

   _____

3. Why does a real witch have slightly larger nose-holes than ordinary people?

   _____

4. In what way are the eyes of a real witch different from yours and mine?

   _____

5. What problems do real witches have with their feet and shoes?

   _____

6. How might someone recognise a witch wearing ordinary shoes?

   _____

7. What type of liquid does a witch's spit resemble? _____

8. Describe how a witch can write with her spit.

   _____

Ⓑ Deeper Thinking

1. Why would it be easier for the young boy to recognise a witch in summer than in winter?

   _____
   _____

2. How do you know that the young boy is an inquisitive child?

   _____
   _____

3. How do you know that his grandmother is taking this conversation seriously?

   _____

4. What kind of person do you think the young boy is? Explain your answer.

   _____
   _____

5. What sentence tells us that Roald Dahl didn't like people smoking cigars?

   _____
   _____

Why do you think the young boy lives with his grandmother?

_____

Suggest a reason why you think his grandmother knows so much about witches and how to recognise them.

_____

C Vocabulary Work: Correct Spellings

There are two words spelled incorrectly in each sentence below.
Ring the words and then write them correctly in the spaces provided.

1. His granmother told him how to recognice a witch. (a) _____ (b) _____
2. A real wich doesn't have finger nales. (a) _____ (b) _____
3. Wigs make the skalp very itshy. (a) _____ (b) _____
4. The smel from them comes ozing out of their skin. (a) _____ (b) _____
5. Children smell absolutly dissgusting to a witch. (a) _____ (b) _____
6. He couldn't belive she was telling him the trut. (a) _____ (b) _____
7. He desided to change the subjext. (a) _____ (b) _____
8. Wiches never have tooes on their feet. (a) _____ (b) _____
9. Witches hav pekuliar eyes. (a) _____ (b) _____
10. You mite see a witch limping slitely. (a) _____ (b) _____
11. A witch has a spit that is as blu as a billberry. (a) _____ (b) _____
12. Witches use there blue spit to rite with. (a) _____ (b) _____
13. Witches wite with old-fassioned pens. (a) _____ (b) _____
14. He was fassinated with her storys about witches. (a) _____ (b) _____
15. This extrct is from a book caled *The Witches*. (a) _____ (b) _____

D Working with Sounds: The Digraph /th/

The /th/ digraph has two separate and distinct sounds:
(a) the **unvoiced** /th/, where you put your tongue between your teeth,
e.g. **th**ink, **th**ird, **th**ank, **th**eory, **th**ief, mo**th**, **th**eatre, **th**ousand.
(b) the **voiced** /th/, where you put your tongue on the roof of your mouth,
e.g. **th**at, **th**is, **th**ese, **th**ose, **th**em, ga**th**er, o**th**er, **th**ey.

Read the words in the word box below and decide whether the /th/ sound is voiced or unvoiced. Write the words in the correct columns in the grid below.

thermal	theatre	threat	thermometer	thief	athlete
thrill	wealthy	thrush	thug	thrash	strength
therapy	throne	third	eighth	those	there
month	rather	either	thing	length	brother

Unvoiced /th/ sound		Voiced /th/ sound	

E Grammar: Direct Speech – Quotation Marks

Direct speech is a report of the exact words used by a speaker or writer. These exact words are placed inside **quotation marks**. Question marks, commas, exclamation marks and full stops are also placed inside the quotation marks, e.g. 'The feet have square ends with no toes on them at all,' said grandmamma. 'Does that make it difficult to walk?' I said.

Rewrite these sentences putting the exact words used inside quotation marks.

1. What else is different about them, Grandmamma? he asked.

   _____

2. The feet, she said. Witches never have toes on their feet.

   _____

3. No toes! I cried. Then, what do they have?

   _____

4. They just have feet, my grandmother said. The feet have square ends with no toes.

   _____

5. Does that make it difficult for them to walk? I asked.

   _____

6. Tell me what else to look for in a witch I said to her after a while.

   _____

7. Extremely uncomfortable, my grandmother said. But she has to put up with it.

   _____

8. Exactly, she said, they even use it to write with.

   _____

F Extension Ideas

Use the library or internet to help you with the following exercise.

1. **Write the titles of four other books written by Roald Dahl.**

   (a) _____

   (b) _____

   (c) _____

   (d) _____

2. **Write the names of four witches from any other stories you have read.**

   (a) _____

   (b) _____

   (c) _____

   (d) _____

G Writing Genre: Narrative Writing

Imagine you met a witch(es) at home or in school. Write the story of what happens in your encounter with the witch(es). Complete the template below.

Title: **The Day I Met a Witch**

Who are the characters in the story? _____

Where does the story take place? _____

When did the story happen? _____

How does the story begin? _____

_____

What problems will the characters face? _____

_____

Resolution: How will things work out? _____

_____

Conclusion: How will the characters feel in the end? _____

_____

Now, write your story.

Title: **The Day I Met a Witch**

_____

_____

_____

_____

_____

_____

_____

_____

_____

H Self Reflection

I was good at: _____

I need to do more work on: _____ Date: _____

A **A Little Light Thinking**

1. How old was Isabel? _____

2. What crop was grown on most farms in Cuba up until 1989? _____

3. What did Iván want to be when he grew up? _____

4. What was Iván's surname? _____

5. Who was the ruler of Cuba at the time? _____

6. What instrument did Isabel play? _____

7. Why did Isabel toss her old baseball cap on the ground?

   _____

8. Describe the buildings in the city.

   _____

9. Where did Isabel part ways with her father and grandfather?

   _____

10. What kind of tune did Isabel play on her trumpet on the promenade?

    _____

B **Deeper Thinking**

1. Why do you think Isabel was barefoot as she always tended to be?

   _____

2. What do you think caused Cuba to hit rock bottom after the fall of the Soviet Union?

   _____

   _____

3. Why did Iván lie about what they were building in their shed?

   _____

   _____

4. How do you think Isabel knew about the punishment for trying to escape to the USA?

   _____

5. What line tells us that Isabel's mother thought Isabel was a good trumpet player?

   _____

   _____

6. Why do you think the only people to give Isabel money were tourists?

   _____

In what way does the political system in Ireland differ to the
political system in Cuba in 1994?

_____

C **Vocabulary Work: Jumbled Sentences**

Unscramble the words to make sentences about the story. Write the sentences.

1. had Isabel hungry scrawny kitten. calico a

   _____

2. was a Her lunch few and a white rice. small pile of beans

   _____

3. beach. bit of the fish on dead found a Iván

   _____

4. and a boat to sail were building a his to the USA. father Iván

   _____

5. Isabel inside for her trumpet. ran

   _____

6. and grandfather Isabel her father Havana. trips into tagging along with on loved

   _____

7. ground. Isabel baseball cap on the tossed her old

   _____

8. was trying Isabel to hear of Cuba the heartbeat music. in her own

   _____

9. trumpet lifted Isabel the lips. to her

   _____

10. older Iván year a was Isabel. than

    _____

D **Working with Sounds: The Diphthongs /ou/ and /ow/**

The diphthongs /ou/ and /ow/ have the same sound, e.g. round, shroud, trousers, crouch, stout, bounce, cow, coward, chowder, powder, crowd, gown, clown.

Insert the diphthongs /ou/ or /ow/ to complete the following sentences.

1. We saw the cl__ __n, upside d__ __n, with a sad fr__ __n on his face.
2. The h__ __nd h__ __led and gr__ __led at the robber who was in her h__ __se.
3. The fl__ __ering plants began to spr__ __t in the gr__ __nd in springtime.
4. N__ __ns are naming words that can be f__ __nd in sentences.
5. There was a large cr__ __d of people sh__ __ting in the t__ __n square.
6. The wise old __ __l is a nocturnal bird of prey and can be br__ __n in colour.
7. Mum mixed the fl__ __r and water in the b__ __l.
8. 'Can you c__ __nt the br__ __n cows on the m__ __nd for me?' asked Sam.
9. The children went __ __tside and the dog gr__ __led at them.
10. 'Please sh__ __t __ __t the five v__ __el s__ __nds,' said the teacher.
11. The st__ __t cl__ __n had a s__ __r apple in his m__ __th.
12. The lady's sp__ __se found a m__ __se running in the h__ __se.
13. 'How high can you c__ __nt al__ __d in one h__ __r?' asked the teacher.

E Grammar: Indirect Speech

Indirect speech is usually used to talk about the past, so we normally change the tense to the past tense. We may use the word *that* to introduce the reported words, e.g.
Direct speech: 'I need your help in the shed,' said his father.
Indirect speech: His father said **that** he needed his help in the shed.
Remember: Quotation marks are **not** used in indirect speech.

Change the direct speech in the following sentences into indirect speech.

1. 'You are not much to look at,' Isabel said to Kitty.

   _____

2. 'I found a bit of dead fish on the beach for the cat,' said Iván to Isabel.

   _____

3. 'The cat needs a name,' Iván said to Isabel.

   _____

4. 'She's a little lion,' said Iván to Isabel.

   _____

5. 'Those are all boys' names!' Isabel said.

   _____

6. 'Iván!' his father called from next door. 'I need help in the shed.'

   _____

7. 'I tossed an old ball cap on the ground,' said Isabel.

   _____

8. 'We are building a doghouse,' said Iván.

   _____

9. 'I am worried that the Castillos will get caught,' stated Isabel.

   _____

10. 'There isn't enough food to feed my kitten,' said Isabel.

    _____

F Extension Ideas

Use the library or internet to help you with the following exercise.

1. **Find Cuba on a map of the world. Describe its location.**

   _____

   _____

2. **Write two interesting facts about Cuba.**

   (a) _____

   (b) _____

3. **Draw the flag of Cuba.**

G Writing Genre: Narrative Writing

Imagine you are in a situation from which you badly need to escape. Research, plan and write the story of your escape from this difficult situation. Complete the template below.

Title: _____

Who are the characters in the story? _____

Where does the story happen? _____

When does the story happen? _____

How does the story start? _____

_____

Problem: What problems will the characters face?_____

_____

Resolution: How will things work out? _____

_____

Conclusion: How do the characters feel in the end? _____

_____

Now, write your story.

Title: _____

_____

_____

_____

_____

_____

_____

_____

_____

_____

H **Self Reflection**

I was good at: _____

I need to do more work on: _____ Date: _____

9 Life in Cuba

A A Little Light Thinking

1. Where in the world is Cuba located?

2. What is the approximate population of Cuba?

3. What is the name of the largest city in Cuba?

4. What does *El Caimá* mean?

5. Why do tourists like to visit Varadero?

6. When did Christopher Columbus arrive on the island?

7. Explain, briefly, what the communist system means.

8. What was the main crop grown in Cuba?

9. What is the most popular sport in Cuba?

10. About how many tourists visit Cuba every year?

B Deeper Thinking

1. Do you think *El Cocodrilo* or *El Caimá* are good names for Cuba? Explain.

2. Do you think September and October would be good times to visit Cuba? Why?

3. Why do Cubans speak Spanish?

4. Why do you think corruption took hold in Cuba in the early 1900s?

5. What sentence tells us that relations have not been good between Cuba and the USA for many years?

6. Why do you think tourism is so important to the Cuban economy?

Write two things that have made Cuba famous and explain why.

(a)

(b)

C Vocabulary Work: Thesaurus Work

Choose the word closest in meaning to the underlined word. Write the words.

corruption	colony	inhabitants	occupation	rugged
tropical	officially	subsidised	dense	dominated

1. Cuba, or the Republic of Cuba as it is <u>formally</u> known, is an island. _____

2. Cuba has a population of more than 11 million <u>citizens</u>. _____

3. The island is mostly flat with <u>jagged</u> hills along the coastal areas. _____

4. Cuba has a(n) <u>equatorial</u> climate. It is very hot and wet at times. _____

5. Christopher Columbus claimed Cuba as a Spanish <u>territory</u> in 1492. _____

6. For decades, <u>dishonesty</u> reigned, with the rich getting richer. _____

7. Fidel Castro grew up in a region <u>controlled</u> by American owned sugar mills. _____

8. Education and health are completely <u>financed</u> by the government. _____

9. Regardless of their <u>job</u>, most Cubans receive similar wages. _____

10. The bee hummingbird is found in the <u>thick</u> forest and woodland areas. _____

D Comprehension Work: Cloze Procedure

Use the words in the word box to complete the story below.

1492	reigned	officially	million	vehicles
Jamaica	colony	Havana	destitute	prime
health	foreign	located	USA	revolutionaries
language	crocodile	Spanish	impossible	independence

Cuba

Cuba, or the Republic of Cuba as it is _____ known, is _____ in the Caribbean Sea. It is to the east of Mexico, south of Florida and the Bahamas, west of Haiti and north of _____ and the Cayman Islands. It is the largest island in the Caribbean and has a population of about 11 _____ people.

Cuba has the shape of a _____ or an alligator on a map. Its capital city is _____ which has a population of about 2.1 million people. Many American _____ from the 1950s are still in use in Cuba. Fidel Castro placed a ban on importing _____ vehicles, so it became nearly _____ to buy a new car.

In _____, Christopher Columbus arrived on the island and claimed it as a _____ territory. It remained a Spanish _____ until the war between Spain and the _____ in 1898, when Cuba became part of the USA. To this day, the official _____ of Cuba is Spanish. Cuba got its _____ in 1902.

Corruption _____ in Cuba until the late 1950s, with the rich getting richer and the poor becoming _____. Fidel Castro led communist _____ in 1959 and took over Cuba. Castro was _____ minister until 2008 when he stood down because of ill _____. His brother, Raul, took over as prime minister.

9 Life in Cuba

E Working with Words: Wordsearch

Ring the following words in the wordsearch.

l	y	z	e	r	u	t	i	n	r	u	f
y	p	a	t	s	i	v	r	u	t	o	o
x	y	f	r	n	y	e	z	r	n	b	s
j	a	r	o	o	n	g	y	n	i	d	f
b	n	u	p	i	o	e	s	i	r	r	s
i	i	i	i	t	t	t	p	i	t	e	s
c	m	t	c	a	z	a	b	u	e	p	r
y	a	b	a	p	k	b	r	r	o	c	e
c	l	a	l	u	r	l	t	r	e	p	w
l	s	y	f	c	h	e	t	x	s	c	o
e	m	e	v	c	z	s	a	x	g	e	l
s	r	c	l	o	t	h	e	s	q	d	f

fruit ↓   flowers ↑

vegetables ↓   birds ↗

clothes →   sports ↙

furniture ←   occupations ↑

trees ↗   animals ↓

bicycles ↓   tropical ↓

F Grammar: Homonyms

Homonyms are words that have the same sound and spelling but different meanings, e.g. **right**: (a) Turn **right**, (b) Everyone has the **right** to live a peaceful life.

Write two meanings for the following homonyms.

1. (a) address: _____

   (b) address: _____

2. (a) club: _____

   (b) club: _____

3. (a) book: _____

   (b) book: _____

4. (a) space: _____

   (b) space: _____

5. (a) fly: _____

   (b) fly: _____

6. (a) blue: _____

   (b) blue: _____

G Extension Ideas

Use the library or internet to help you with the following exercise.

Write the names of four more islands in the Caribbean Sea.

1. _____   2. _____

3. _____   4. _____

H **Writing Genre: Persuasive Writing**

Plan and write a persuasive argument supporting or disagreeing with the belief that a communist system of government would not be the fairest type of system.

Complete the template below.

Title: **A Communist System of Government Would Not Be the Fairest Type of System**

State your point of view: _____

_____

Reason 1: _____

_____

Reason 2: _____

_____

Reason 3: _____

_____

Conclusion: Give a summary of your main points. _____

_____

_____

Finally, I think that I have shown… _____

_____

_____

Now, write your persuasive argument.

Title: **A Communist System of Government Would Not Be the Fairest Type of System**

_____

_____

_____

_____

_____

_____

_____

_____

_____

1 Self Reflection

I was good at: _____

I need to do more work on: _____ Date: _____

A A Little Light Thinking

1. What did Belle think the *things* coming out of the ground looked like at first?

2. Who was Belle's mother? _____

3. Who did Belle think had cursed the castle with spiderwebs?

4. What did the webbing that had grown over the gates feel like?

5. Describe the wolves.

6. What slowed down Phillipe's gallop? _____

7. Why did Phillipe buck wildly and knock Belle off his back?

8. Who arrived to save Belle from the wolves? _____

B Deeper Thinking

1. What popular fairy tale does this story remind you of?

2. Why do you think Belle wanted to escape from the Beast? _____

3. In fairy tales, the main character always has a problem. Who is the main character and what problem does he/she encounter in this story? _____

4. What fairy tale element do you think the wolves represent in this story?

5. Why didn't Belle stop Phillipe from running over the snowy pond?

6. Fairy tales often teach a lesson. In your opinion, what lesson does this story teach?

CHALLENGE

Fairy tales often have happy endings. In two sentences, write a possible happy ending to this story.

(a) _____

(b) _____

C Vocabulary Work: Crossword

Complete the crossword using the clues below. All the words are in the story.

ACROSS

5. Sudden, uncontrollable fear or anxiety
6. Not smoothly or gracefully
7. Relatives or predecessors
12. The ability to acquire and apply knowledge and skills
13. A woman who uses magic to put someone under a spell
14. Not giving way to pressure

DOWN

1. A feeling of disgust
2. A formal announcement
3. Making a high-pitched piercing cry or sound
4. To become partly or wholly incapable of movement
5. Outer boundary
8. Not willing to do something and therefore slow to do it
9. Trembled with fear
10. In a way that shows great happiness or joy at a victory or achievement
11. Struggling or staggering clumsily in mud or water

D Grammar: Homophones

Homophones are words that sound the same but have different spellings and meanings, e.g. course → coarse. I am attending an art course. / Coarse is another word for rough.

Write each word in a sentence to show its meaning.

1. (a) seen: _____

   (b) scene: _____

2. (a) bridal: _____

   (b) bridle: _____

3. (a) lair: _____

   (b) layer: _____

4. (a) tale: _____

   (b) tail: _____

5. (a) manner: _____

   (b) manor: _____

6. (a) reins: _____

   (b) rains: _____

E **Working with Sounds: Suffixes -cial and -tial**

The suffixes -cial and -tial have a /shal/ sound as in social, special, partial, potential, etc.
Rule 1: Use -cial after a vowel, e.g. social, facial, racial, glacial, official, artificial.
Rule 2: Use -tial after a consonant, as in essential, influential, confidential, etc.
Exceptions: controversial, financial, commercial, provincial, initial, spatial, palatial.

Insert the correct -cial or -tial word from the word box in the sentences below.

martial	special	official	initials	residential
financial	social	potential	substantial	palatial
commercial	essential	controversial	artificial	partial

1. The _____ sponsor of the football team provided money to buy jerseys.

2. Judo is a _____ art and also an Olympic sport.

3. An accountant is a person whose job is to keep _____ accounts.

4. The _____ GAA, stand for *Gaelic Athletic Association*.

5. An area where people live is often referred to as a _____ area.

6. Tickets to a concert can cost a _____ amount of money.

7. Tom changes the channels on the TV during the _____ breaks.

8. 'He is showing great _____ as an artist,' said the teacher.

9. 'It is _____ that you study hard in order to pass your exams,' said her mum.

10. The referee made a _____ decision by sending off the team captain.

11. VIPs get _____ treatment because they are thought to be important.

12. The flowers in the vase are _____, meaning they are not real.

13. A house as luxurious as a palace can be described as _____.

14. The boy only gave a _____ answer to the question.

15. Dogs are _____ animals and make very good pets.

F **Extension Ideas**

Use the library or internet to help you with the following exercise.

1. **Define what a fairy tale is.**

    _____

2. **Research the main elements of a fairy tale. List five elements below and describe how each is present in this story.**

    (a) _____

    (b) _____

    (c) _____

    (d) _____

    (e) _____

10 As Old as Time — A Twisted Tale

G **Writing Genre: Persuasive Writing**

Research, plan and write your persuasive argument that fairy tales are still relevant for teaching children moral lessons about life. Complete the template below.

Title: **Fairy Tales Are Still Relevant for Teaching Children Moral Lessons About Life**

Introduction: Write a statement giving your opinion.

_____

Assertion: I have several reasons for arguing this point of view.

Reason 1: _____

_____

Reason 2: _____

_____

Reason 3: _____

_____

Reason 4: _____

_____

Conclusion: Give a summary of your main points. _____

_____

Finally, I think that I have shown… _____

_____

_____

Now, write your persuasive argument.

Title: **Fairy Tales Are Still Relevant for Teaching Children Moral Lessons About Life**

_____

_____

_____

_____

_____

_____

H **Self Reflection**

I was good at: _____

I need to do more work on: _____ Date: _____

A A Little Light Thinking

1. What happened to most of the men who died in the trenches?

   _____

2. How many men did the Canadians lose in the battle of Passchendaele?

   _____

3. What was the area between the trenches called? _____

4. What did the German soldier say they were having for Christmas dinner?

   _____

5. Who was given the flask of rum? _____

6. Who appeared from the reserve trench? _____

B Deeper Thinking

1. What do you think is meant by a *Blighty Ticket*?

   _____

2. Why do you think the men's belief that the war would end began to fade?

   _____

   _____

3. Who do you think Kaiser Bill was?

   _____

4. Name three types of trench mentioned in the story.

   (a) _____   (b) _____   (c) _____

5. Why do you think the soldiers had to ration their supplies?

   _____

   _____

6. What do you think is meant by the line: *We were back at stalemate*?

   _____

7. The soldier threw a flask of rum over to the Germans. Write two bad effects that drinking alcohol can have on people.

   (a) _____

   (b) _____

8. Write two bad effects that smoking tobacco can have on people.

   (a) _____

   (b) _____

CHALLENGE

Write the names of eight countries that were involved in World War I.

(a) _____   (b) _____   (c) _____   (d) _____

(e) _____   (f) _____   (g) _____   (h) _____

C **Vocabulary Work: Jumbled Letters**

1. **Use the clues to help you unscramble the letters to make words from the story.**

   (a) A long narrow hole dug by soldiers: (tchenr)   t_____

   (b) A lengthy, bloody fight: (ttable)   _____

   (c) A concrete fort used as an outpost: (oxbllip)   p_____

   (d) A dessert made from milk and eggs: (arusctd)   _____

   (e) A person who serves in the army: (ldreios)   _____

   (f) Prepared leaves used in cigarettes: (ooaccbt)   t_____

   (g) A popular game played with a bat: (ccirtek)   _____

   (h) An officer in the army: (antieleunt)   l_____

   (i) Day to commemorate the birth of Jesus: (masCsirht)   _____

   (j) The 12th month of the year: (rebmecDe)   _____

2. **Unscramble the letters to make words from the story.**

   (a) ortyicv = v_____   (b) nuowded = w_____

   (c) ertbtade = b_____   (d) arttree = r_____

   (e) mmicnniotauoc = c_____   (f) nirdftig = d_____

   (g) nneorfilt = f_____   (h) ionarts = r_____

D **Working with Sounds: Prefixes dis- and de-**

The **prefixes dis-** and **de-** are placed at the start of words to make new words,
e.g. order → **dis**order / activate → **de**activate.

1. **Add the prefix dis- or de- to the following to make words.**

_____scend	_____duct	_____belief	_____respect	_____connect
_____count	_____grade	_____ficient	_____order	_____qualify

2. **Put each of the above words in the correct sentence below.**

   (a) She stared in _____ at the damage done to her car.

   (b) The soldier began to _____ the wooden ladder into the muddy trench.

   (c) The sergeant felt that the lieutenant had total _____ for what he was saying.

   (d) 'Please do not _____ the lead to the printer or it won't work,' she said.

   (e) The referee will _____ anyone who does not obey the rules of the game.

   (f) There was great _____ in the factory after a large delivery of goods arrived.

   (g) The workers were entitled to a 10 percent _____ on all their purchases.

   (h) Scratches on the camera lens will _____ the quality of the photo.

   (i) The old lady was _____ in calcium, so her bones broke easily.

   (j) The boss decided to _____ the cost of the broken window from the
        girl's wages as she was very careless with her work.

3. **Write two more words beginning with the prefix dis- and de-.**

   (a) _____   (b) _____

   (c) _____   (d) _____

E Grammar: Homographs

Remember: **Homographs** are words that look and are spelled the same but have different sounds and meanings, e.g. **wound**: (a) The young soldier died from his **wound** in the muddy trenches, (b) The lady **wound** the old grandfather clock in the sitting room.

Write each word in a sentence to show two different meanings.

1. (a) live: _____
   (b) live: _____

2. (a) refuse: _____
   (b) refuse: _____

3. (a) survey: _____
   (b) survey: _____

4. (a) produce: _____
   (b) produce: _____

5. (a) project: _____
   (b) project: _____

6. (a) moped: _____
   (b) moped: _____

7. (a) close: _____
   (b) close: _____

8. (a) excuse: _____
   (b) excuse: _____

9. (a) content: _____
   (b) content: _____

10. (a) record: _____
    (b) record: _____

F Extension Ideas

Use the library or internet to help you with the following exercise.

1. Write four interesting facts about conditions in the trenches during World War I.

   (a) _____

   (b) _____

   (c) _____

   (d) _____

2. Write the names of three animals that were used to help during the war.

   (a) _____ (b) _____ (c) _____

G **Writing Genre: Writing to Socialise**

Imagine you are Jim. Write a letter to your family, telling them about life in the trenches on Christmas Day and what you hope will happen in the future. Complete the template.

Address: _____

_____

_____

_____

Date: _____

Greeting: _____

_____

Paragraph 1: _____

_____

_____

_____

Paragraph 2: _____

_____

_____

_____

Paragraph 3: _____

_____

_____

_____

Farewell: _____

Sign off: _____

Now, write your letter.

_____

_____

_____

_____

_____ ,

_____

_____

_____

_____

_____

_____

_____

_____

_____

_____

_____

_____

_____

_____

H Self Reflection

I was good at: _____

I need to do more work on: _____ Date: _____

A A Little Light Thinking

1. Name three countries that were on the side of the Central Powers.

    (a) _____ (b) _____ (c) _____

2. What is Lord Kitchener saying to the British people in the recruitment poster?

    _____

3. Why were tanks invented? _____

4. How many Allied aeroplanes did the Red Baron shoot down? _____

5. Name three terrible battles that took place during World War I.

    (a) _____ (b) _____ (c) _____

6. What work did the women do while the men were away at war?

    _____

7. Where did the *Lusitania* sink? _____

8. What was used to sink the *Lusitania*? _____

9. On what date does Armistice Day take place each year? _____

10. How many people in total are estimated to have died due to World War I? _____

B Deeper Thinking

1. Why do you think World War I was the worst war the world had ever known?

    _____

2. Write two sentences describing the trenches.

    (a) _____

    (b) _____

3. Give two reasons why you think there was a truce on Christmas Day in 1914.

    (a) _____

    (b) _____

4. Why do you think aerial battles were known as *dogfights*? _____

    _____

5. In what ways might it have been dangerous to work in a munitions factory?

    _____

    _____

CHALLENGE

Why might people have thought that World War I was the war to end all wars?

_____

_____

12 World War I

C **Vocabulary Work: Dictionary Meanings**

Continue these short sentences to show the dictionary meaning of the underlined words.

1. An <u>onlooker</u> _____

2. Young men <u>enlisted</u> _____

3. The <u>assassination</u> _____

4. The <u>disastrous</u> _____

5. Modern <u>machinery</u> _____

6. The muddy <u>terrain</u> _____

7. The <u>viewers</u> _____

8. The <u>conflict</u> _____

9. The <u>truce</u> _____

10. The French <u>infantry</u> _____

11. <u>Eventually</u>, _____

12. <u>Unidentified</u> soldiers _____

13. A <u>sombre</u> _____

D **Comprehension Work: Cloze Procedure**

Use the words in the word box to complete the story below.

Allies	lasted	amputated	Italy	trenches
France	poisonous	Austria	soldiers	*Lusitania*
citizens	bombs	armistice	torpedoed	tanks
Central	reconnaissance	passengers	assassination	developed

World War I

World War I began in 1914 and _____ for over four years. World War I began after the _____ of Franz Ferdinand and his wife Sophie. The two sides in this horrific war were the Allies and the _____ Powers. The Allies were the countries of Britain, _____ and Russia. The Central Powers were the countries of Germany, Italy and _____ -Hungary. _____ changed sides in 1915.

Much of World War I was fought in muddy _____. Soldiers shared these trenches with huge rats and many soldiers _____ a condition known as trench foot. Their infected feet often had to be _____. Sometimes, when _____ were shot in these trenches, their bodies were left to rot where they fell.

Terrible, new weapons were invented during World War I. The Allies used armoured _____ to cross the muddy terrain. The Central Powers used _____ gas to attack the soldiers of the _____. About 70 different types of aeroplane were used for carrying out _____ missions and dropping deadly _____.

The USA entered World War I on 6th April 1917. This was after a German submarine _____ a British passenger ship, the _____, off the coast of Cork. Over 1,000 _____ on board died, of whom 128 were American _____. World War I ended on the 11th hour of the 11th day of the 11th month in 1918. An _____ was signed by both sides.

E Grammar: Personal Pronouns

A **personal pronoun** is a word that takes the place of a noun. The personal pronouns are as follows: **I, you, he, she, it, we, they, me, us, her, him** and **them**.

1. **Write a suitable pronoun to complete the following sentences.**

   (a) 'Your country needs _____,' said Lord Kitchener during World War I.

   (b) '_____ want to enlist in the army and fight for freedom,' said Tom.

   (c) Soldiers had to face heavy fire if _____ tried to cross No Man's Land.

   (d) _____ is estimated that between 17 and 19 million people died because of World War I, many from hunger and disease.

   (e) 'I hope _____ all get to visit your grandfather on Saturday,' said Dad.

   (f) The Lieutenant saw _____ all playing football in No Man's Land.

   (g) 'I really like my aunt because _____ is always very nice to _____,' said Sofia.

   (h) _____ is a brilliant soldier. His parents are very proud of _____.

   (i) Elaine rode in the car beside _____ husband on their journey to Cork.

   (j) We were delighted when the old man gave a talk to _____ on World War I.

2. **Read the information in brackets. Then write the correct personal pronoun in the following sentences.**

   (a) _____ likes reading adventure books in the library. (Carmel)

   (b) _____ are going to Cork on the train. (My sister and I)

   (c) _____ camped beside the lake with his friends. (David)

   (d) _____ wear a school uniform every day except Friday. (The pupils)

   (e) '_____ are over there on the shelf,' said the teacher. (The books)

   (f) _____ built a nest in the oak tree near the estuary. (The bird)

   (g) _____ was one of the best Formula 1 drivers ever. (Ayrton Senna)

   (h) _____ are going swimming in the pool after school today. (The children)

   (i) _____ was born in Germany but _____ died in Holland. (Anne Frank)

   (j) _____ hope to go travelling in the summer with our family. (Tom and I)

F Extension Ideas

Use the library or internet to help you with the following exercise.

1. **Write four interesting facts about the *Battle of the Somme*.**

   (a) _____

   (b) _____

   (c) _____

   (d) _____

2. **Write two interesting facts about Edith Cavell who made a significant contribution to the war effort in Britain.**

   (a) _____

   (b) _____

G Writing Genre: Writing to Socialise

You are a soldier fighting for the Allies. Imagine the war has just ended.
Write a postcard to a friend or family member telling them about what has happened.
Complete the template below.

Name of friend/family member: _____

Street and number: _____

Town: _____

County: _____

Postal code: _____

Country: _____

Date: _____

Greeting: _____

Paragraph 1: _____

_____

_____

Paragraph 2: _____

_____

_____

Paragraph 3: _____

_____

_____

Farewell: _____

Sign off: _____

Now, write your postcard.

H **Self Reflection**

I was good at: _____

I need to do more work on: _____ Date: _____

13 A Horse Called El Dorado

A A Little Light Thinking

1. How did Pepe feel when he thought of the Muisca Indian warriors?

    He felt a bit braver.

2. What did he see ahead as the path widened to a sandy expanse?

    He seen crocodiles as the path widened.

3. Who did Pepe fear might shatter the quietness of the jungle?

    He feared the AGRA guerrillas jeeps and music would shatter it.

4. Who was responsible for the murder of Gonzales? The AGRA guerrillas were responsible.

5. How many attempts did it take Pepe to get to the great silent tree? It took 3 attempts.

6. What could Pepe hear Paul Rooke's voice saying in his mind?

    "You are responsible for over ten thousand in banknotes, kid!"

7. What did he use to dust the lanes of footprints that he and his horse had made?

    He used a branch with a wide fan of long leaves.

8. What did Pepe say would keep away small animals during the night?

    Pepe said El Dorado's snoring would keep small animals away during the night.

B Deeper Thinking

1. Why do you think Pepe couldn't think of his mother as he galloped through the jungle?

    I think he couldn't think of her because he was scared in case he never seen her again.

2. Give two reasons why you think Pepe was going on this secret mission at night-time.

    (a) He went at night so no one would see him.

    (b) He went because the rhyme said 'go there at night but never at day.'

3. What do you think Pepe meant when he said: *This was a climb for a man, not a mere boy*?

    I think he meant the climb was suitable for grown men, not little boys.

4. How did Pepe and his horse, El Dorado, communicate with each other?

    They communicated through body language.

5. Why do you think Pepe's horse was called El Dorado?

    I think he was called that because he was a golden horse and El Dorado is the name of the lost city of gold.

6. What do you think will happen next in the story? Explain your reasoning.

    I think someone who was travelling on the river might find him because he was resting near the river.

CHALLENGE

Name three small animals that might have attacked them in the jungle.

(a) _____ (b) _____ (c) _____

C **Vocabulary Work: Synonyms**

Rewrite the sentences using the word closest in meaning to the underlined word.

1. The boy looked <u>confused</u> when he saw the exam paper. (happy / puzzled / alert)

   The boy looked puzzled when he saw the exam paper.

2. The guard was <u>wary</u> of the violent prisoner. (trusting / believing / suspicious)

   The guard was suspicious of the violent prisoner.

3. The egg was <u>intact</u> even though it fell from the nest. (smashed / unbroken / broken)

   The egg was unbroken even though it fell from the nest.

4. The camel <u>gulped</u> down the water at the oasis. (sipped / guzzled / tasted)

   The camel guzzled down the water at the oasis.

5. The train came to a <u>halt</u> at the station. (start / standstill / beginning)

   The train came to a standstill at the station.

6. It was hard to <u>concentrate</u> with the loud music playing. (stray / drift / focus)

   It was hard to focus with the loud music playing.

D **Working with Sounds: Prefixes en-, ex- and extra-**

1. **Write the following words in a short sentence to show their meaning.**
   You may use your dictionary to help you.

   (a) external: _____

   (b) encounter: _____

   (c) exit: _____

   (d) extraordinary: _____

   (e) enable: _____

   (f) excursion: _____

2. **Write the noise each animal makes. Use each word from the word box only once.**

squeak	purr	laugh	trumpet	hiss	whinny
buzz	grunt	gobble	roar	hoot	growl
moo	quack	coo	chatter	click	croak

(a) horse			(b) lion	
(c) cow			(d) cat	
(e) owl			(f) pigeon	
(g) bee			(h) pig	
(i) duck			(j) hyena	
(k) turkey			(l) dolphin	
(m) elephant			(n) frog	
(o) monkey			(p) snake	
(q) bear			(r) mouse	

E Grammar: Adjectives

1. Write the adjectives from the word box under the correct headings below.

terrified	irate	stunning	elated	huge
cross	delighted	enraged	massive	spooked
afraid	resentful	ecstatic	alarmed	exquisite
appealing	petrified	large	thrilled	pleased
handsome	agitated	immense	enormous	gorgeous

Scared	Happy	Angry	Big	Pretty
terrified	elated	irate	huge	stunning
spooked	delighted	cross	massive	exquisite
afraid	ecstatic	enraged	large	appealing
alarmed	thrilled	agitated	immense	handsome
petrified	pleased	resentful	enormous	gorgeous

2. Write the adjectives in each sentence.

(a) He rode along a long, dark path.   (i) _long_   (ii) _dark_

(b) The crocodiles shuffled on their small, webbed legs.   (i) _small_   (ii) _webbed_

(c) He gulped great bellyfuls of cold water.   (i) _great_   (ii) _cold_

(d) He chose a good, strong branch in the forest.   (i) _good_   (ii) _strong_

(e) He found a broad branch with wide leaves.   (i) _broad_   (ii) _wide_

(f) He rested his sore, thick neck on the ground.   (i) _sore_   (ii) _thick_

F Extension Ideas

Use the library or internet to help you with the following exercise.

1. Write four interesting facts about crocodiles.

(a) _____

(b) _____

(c) _____

(d) _____

2. Name six birds you might see in the jungle.

(a) _____ (b) _____ (c) _____

(d) _____ (e) _____ (f) _____

G **Writing Genre: Procedural Writing**

In the story, Pepe had to follow the instructions to find the commune's secret tree. He brought food for the journey in his bandana. Imagine that you are going on a picnic with your friend. Plan and write a recipe for (a) granola bars and (b) chocolate muffins. Write the step-by-step procedure for making granola bars below.

(a) Title: **Recipe for Granola Bars**

Ingredients: _____

_____

Requirements (equipment needed): _____

_____

Method: Step-by-step instructions

Step 1: _____

_____

Step 2: _____

_____

Step 3: _____

_____

Step 4: _____

_____

Step 5: _____

_____

Step 6: _____

_____

Step 7: _____

_____

Did you achieve your goal? _____

Now, write the step-by-step procedure for making chocolate muffins.

(b) Title: **Recipe for Chocolate Muffins**

Ingredients: _____

_____

Requirements (equipment needed): _____

_____

Method: Step-by-step instructions

Step 1: _____

_____

Step 2: _____

_____

Step 3: _____

_____

Step 4: _____

_____

Step 5: _____

_____

Step 6: _____

_____

Step 7: _____

_____

Did you achieve your goal? _____

H **Self Reflection**

I was good at: _____

I need to do more work on: _____ Date: _____

A A Little Light Thinking

1. Describe Prim's cat._____

2. What is on top of the chain-link fence? _____

3. What was the nickname for District 12? _____

4. Who did Katniss meet in the woods? _____

5. What three predators mentioned lived in the woods?

   (a) _____ (b) _____ (c) _____

6. Where did the men and the women in the area work? _____

7. What animal used to follow Katniss around in the woods?

   _____

8. Gale didn't pay money for the bread in the bakery. What did it cost him?

   _____

9. Why does Katniss say that Gale could be her brother?

   _____

10. With what does Gale slice the bread?_____

B Deeper Thinking

1. Why do you think their district was nicknamed *the Seam*?

   _____

2. Why do you think Katniss only smiled when she was in the woods?

   _____

3. What do you think the people usually traded on the black market?

   _____

   _____

4. Why do you think the electrified chain-link fence was not always working?

   _____

   _____

5. Write three words and one phrase that tell us Katniss didn't like to show her feelings.

   (a) _____ (b) _____ (c) _____

   (d) _____

CHALLENGE

Describe Gale's appearance and personality.

_____

_____

C Vocabulary Work: Dictionary Meanings

1. Write the dictionary meaning of the following words.

   (a) rebellion: _____

   (b) explosion: _____

   (c) penalties: _____

   (d) indifferent: _____

   (e) venomous: _____

   (f) sentimental: _____

   (g) regretted: _____

   (h) alternative: _____

   (i) illegal: _____

   (j) resemble: _____

2. Write the following words in short sentences to show their meanings.

   (a) threaten: _____

   (b) entrails: _____

   (c) enclosing: _____

   (d) officials: _____

   (e) severest: _____

   (f) expression: _____

   (g) company: _____

   (h) mimics: _____

   (i) related: _____

   (j) delicate: _____

D Working with Sounds: Prefixes re-, pro-, en-, in-, ex- and dis-

1. Write the prefix re-, pro-, en-, in-, ex- or dis- to make words from the story.

   (a) ____sisting   (b) ____members   (c) ____tect   (d) ____closing   (e) ____trieve

   (f) ____plosion   (g) ____different   (h) ____pression   (i) ____semble   (j) ____cussing

2. Write four words of your own beginning with the prefix pre-.

   (a) _____ (b) _____ (c) _____ (d) _____

3. Write four words of your own beginning with the prefix pro-.

   (a) _____ (b) _____ (c) _____ (d) _____

4. Cross out every second letter to find four words beginning with pre- or pro-.

   p c r d e g c f e t d y e g p s r k o s g u r w e m s u s g p f r m e s t w e n x y t g p s r k o f f h i g t

   (a) _____ (b) _____ (c) _____ (d) _____

E Grammar: Demonstrative and Interrogative Pronouns

A **demonstrative pronoun** points out or identifies a noun without naming the noun.
Demonstrative pronouns include **this**, **that**, **these**, **those**.
Others examples of demonstrative pronouns are **none**, **nobody**, **neither**.
An **interrogative pronoun** is used to ask a question: **who**, **whom**, **what**, **which**, **whose**.

1. **Complete each sentence with the correct demonstrative pronoun.**

   (a) I can tell that _____ is a freshly baked loaf. (those / this)

   (b) 'Do all of _____ people work in the mines?' she asked. (that / those)

   (c) '_____ is absolutely beautiful!' she exclaimed. (Those / This)

   (d) '_____ is my absolute favourite of them all,' he said. (Those / That)

   (e) _____ all sneaked under the wire. (That / These)

   (f) 'Bring _____ home with you?' he said, pointing to the bread. (this / those)

   (g) 'Do you know _____ paths in the woods?' she enquired? (that / these)

   (h) '_____ is a list of the reaping names,' he said. (Those / This)

   (i) _____ of the two boys was listening to the teacher. (None / Nobody / Neither)

   (j) _____ of the concert-goers at the back could hear the band.
        (None / Nobody / Neither)

2. **Ring the pronouns in the following. Write if they are demonstrative or interrogative.**

   (a) 'That is the last thing I will say,' said the angry man.   _____

   (b) 'At what times will the games actually begin?' she asked.   _____

   (c) 'To whom does this cat belong?' asked the vet.   _____

   (d) 'These are all going on sale next week,' she said.   _____

   (e) 'We should take those clothes in from the line,' he said.   _____

   (f) 'Which of the coats do you prefer?' he inquired.   _____

   (g) 'Whose car is this?' asked the forecourt attendant.   _____

   (h) 'This was the first time I saw him,' said the witness.   _____

   (i) 'Please give these to Pauric,' said Maria.   _____

   (i) 'This is absolutely beautiful,' said Jamie.   _____

F Extension Ideas

Create a profile for a fictional citizen of Panem.

1. What is your citizen's name? _____

2. How old is he/she? _____

3. Describe him/her. _____

   _____

4. In what district does he/she live? _____

5. Is he/she rich or poor? _____

6. How many people live in the house with him/her? _____

G **Writing Genre: Procedural Writing**

In *The Hunger Games*, people compete against each other in different games in order to survive. Write the step-by-step instructions for how to play your two favourite games. Complete the step-by-step procedure below.

Game 1

Title: _____

Requirements (equipment needed): _____

_____

Method: Step-by-step instructions

Step 1: _____

_____

Step 2: _____

_____

Step 3: _____

_____

Step 4: _____

_____

Step 5: _____

_____

Step 6: _____

_____

Step 7: _____

_____

Step 8: _____

_____

Did you achieve your goal? _____

Game 2

Title: _____

Requirements (equipment needed): _____
_____

Method: Step-by-step instructions

Step 1: _____
_____

Step 2: _____
_____

Step 3: _____
_____

Step 4: _____
_____

Step 5: _____
_____

Step 6: _____
_____

Step 7: _____
_____

Step 8: _____
_____

Did you achieve your goal? _____

H Self Reflection

I was good at: _____

I need to do more work on: _____ Date: _____

15 Great Survivors

Ⓐ A Little Light Thinking

1. In what American city is the Pentagon? _____

2. To what floor in the World Trade Centre had Genelle Guzman-McMillan descended when the building collapsed? _____

3. For how long was she trapped under the wreckage before she was rescued?

   _____

4. What method did Poon Lim use to collect rainwater while adrift at sea?

   _____

5. Over what country did the explosion on board Flight 367 occur? _____

6. Who survived the Flight 367 accident? _____

7. To what did the air safety investigators attribute Vesna Vulović's survival?

   _____

8. What triggered the tsunami in Indonesia on 26th December 2004?

   _____

Ⓑ Deeper Thinking

1. What is meant by the phrase: *coordinated attacks*? _____

   _____

2. Why do you think the occupants of the Word Trade Centre were initially told to remain where they were? _____

   _____

3. Why do you think the *SS Ben Lomand* merchant ship was torpedoed in 1942?

   _____

4. Why might ships' crews have failed to rescue Poon Lim during his time adrift?

   _____

5. What do you think are the main threats that a tsunami poses to a coastal area?

   (a) _____

   (b) _____

6. Chance can play a major part in surviving against the odds. What chance events led to Vesna Vulović's survival? _____

   _____

CHALLENGE

Many tourists now visit Ground Zero in New York. (a) Where exactly is Ground Zero? (b) Why do tourists like to visit this place?

(a) _____

(b) _____

C Vocabulary Work: Dictionary Meanings

Use your dictionary to find the meaning of the following words.

1. magnitude: The magnitude of something is its great size or importance.
2. survivor: someone who lived through great danger or difficulty
3. provisions: The provision of something is the act of making it available to people.
4. merchant: a trader who imports and exports goods.
5. depressurised: _____
6. fractured: a crack or break in something, especially a bone.
7. initial: first, or at the beginning
8. disaster: an event or accident that caused great distress or destruction.
9. astonishing: If something astonishes you, it surprises you very much.
10. vacationing: the period between academic terms at a university or college.
11. investigate: To investigate something is to try to find out all the facts about it.
12. sustained: To sustain something means to continue it for a period of time.
13. submerged: To submerge means to go beneath the surface of a liquid.
14. medic: _____
15. explosion: sudden violent burst of energy, for example one caused by a bomb.

D Comprehension Work: Cloze Procedure

Use the words in the word box to complete the story below.

earthquakes	Ocean	travel	life	detected
treatment	land	magnitude	tsunami	technology
water	coast	survived	Richter	train
countries	December	damage	least	earthquake

Tsunami

A tsunami is often referred to as a _train_ wave. Most tsunamis are caused by underwater _earthquakes_ but not all undersea earthquakes cause tsunamis. An earthquake has to have a _magnitude_ of 7.5 on the Richter scale for it to cause a tsunami. About 90 percent of all tsunamis occur in the Pacific _Ocean_. A tsunami can _travel_ at speeds of up to 800 km/h, which is about as fast as a jet flies. It can take only a few hours for a _tsunami_ to travel across an entire ocean.

When a tsunami hits a coastline, it can cause great destruction and loss of _life_. Many tsunamis can now be _detected_ before they reach _land_ with the use of modern _technology_. Loss of life can now be greatly minimised.

On 26th _December_ 2004, an _earthquake_ occurred off the _coast_ of Sumatra in Indonesia, measuring 9.1 on the _Richter_ scale. This caused a tsunami to hit a dozen _countries_, with Indonesia, Sri Lanka and Thailand sustaining the most _damage_. At _least_ 225,000 people were killed. The lack of food, clean drinking _water_ and proper medical _treatment_ led to the deaths of many who had _survived_ the initial disaster.

15 Great Survivors

E **Grammar: Antonyms**

Antonyms are words that are opposite in meaning, e.g. friend → enemy / natural → unnatural.

Match the words with their antonyms on the right.

courageous ●	● light	damage ●	● unexpected
smooth ●	● united	sank ●	● fatality
boring ●	● shallow	caught ●	● enemy
descended ●	● arrived	possible ●	● east
departed ●	● rough	death ●	● repair
separated ●	● earlier	able ●	● floated
heavy ●	● few	west ●	● impossible
deep ●	● interesting	friend ●	● life
later ●	● cowardly	survivor ●	● unable
many ●	● ascended	expected ●	● released

F **Extension Work**

Use the library or internet to help you with the following exercise.

Research an account of a person or people who survived the impossible.
Write six interesting facts about his/her ordeal.

(a) _____

_____

(b) _____

_____

(c) _____

_____

(d) _____

_____

(e) _____

_____

(f) _____

_____

G Writing Genre: Free Writing

You are one of the people in this picture. In a genre of your choice, write for 15 minutes describing what will happen to you and the other people in the picture.

Title: A Stormy Sea

We were on holidays in a campervan. We were looking for a place to stay when my friend, Sarah, found the perfect place. It was a little town by the sea. "Brilliant!" I squealed. "I love the ocean!" Sarah drove us there. Me and my other friend, Kyle, sat in the back of the van. I must have fallen asleep, as I woke when I heard the sound of the sea. Sarah parked the van right by the sea. "Okay, everyone out!" She yelled. We hopped out of the van.

We were very excited. We decided to get some ice-cream, so we locked the van and left. While we walked to the ice cream van, the weather changed. It became very windy. "I don't think getting ice-cream is a great idea now," said Kyle "Let's go back." "Fine." Sarah said. The weather was getting worse so we started to run. We were getting close to the van.

H **Self Reflection**

I was good at: _____

I need to do more work on: _____ Date: _____

A A Little Light Thinking

1. How did James feel when he entered the water? _____

2. Where had James seen Leo Butcher recently? _____

3. What did Hellebore say that the loser of the race had to give him? _____

4. What was Hellebore's first name? _____

5. How many widths did the boys have to swim underwater in the race? _____

6. What did James think about that made him shudder? _____

7. What did James see under the water? _____

8. What did Hellebore do to James when he tried to get out of the water?

   _____

9. What sentence tells us what country Hellebore was originally from?

   _____

10. Where did Hellebore finally end up? _____

B Deeper Thinking

1. What do you think *the cup* was?

   _____

2. Why do you think the gang backed up Hellebore?

   _____

   _____

3. Do you think Leo Butcher wanted to race against James? Explain.

   _____

   _____

4. Give three examples of where Hellebore is mean to James and Leo.

   (a) _____

   (b) _____

   (c) _____

5. What do you think the pale shape that James thought he glimpsed under the water was?

   _____

How does the author convey James' panic that he might drown?

_____

_____

16 Silverfin – Young James Bond

C **Vocabulary: Dictionary Meanings**

Write the words from the story that are described in the clues.

1. The light of the sun: s_____
2. A game played with a bat and ball: c_____
3. Measure of warmth or coldness: t_____
4. Another word meaning evil: s_____
5. Two sac-like respiratory organs: l_____
6. Colourless, odourless gas used in breathing: o_____
7. A citizen of the USA: A_____
8. Warnings: t_____
9. A public musical performance: c_____
10. cover/cringe/grimace: w_____
11. The top part of the water: s_____
12. Something horrible or disgusting: v_____
13. A large, aquatic reptile with a hard shell: t_____
14. The person crowned winner of a competition: c_____
15. A continuous action, method or operation: p_____

D **Working with Sounds: Prefixes in- and inter-**

Write the prefix in- and inter- to make words. Then, write the dictionary meaning of each word.

1. _____appropriate: _____
2. _____lude: _____
3. _____sect: _____
4. _____attentive: _____
5. _____come: _____
6. _____ternational: _____
7. _____vene: _____
8. _____humane: _____
9. _____credible: _____
10. _____view: _____
11. _____advisable: _____
12. _____rupt: _____
13. _____fere: _____
14. _____visible: _____
15. _____curable: _____

E Grammar: Verb Tenses

A **verb** is an action or doing word that we use in different tenses. The tense tells us when the action occurred. A verb can be used in the past, present or future tenses. Two other tenses are the **past participle** and the **present participle**. The past participle is used to tell when the action was completed, e.g. I **have run** to the school. The present participle is used to tell us that the action is still happening, e.g. I **am running** to school at the moment.

Complete the following table.

Past tense	Present tense	Future tense	Present participle	Past participle
I held	I hold	I will hold	I am holding	I have held
I stood	I stand	I will stand	I am standing	I have stood
I got	I get	I will get	I am getting	I have gotten
I kept	I keep	I will keep	I am keeping	I have kept
I won	I win	I will win	I am winning	I have won
I understood	I understand	I will understand	I am understanding	I have understood
I came	I come	I will come	I am coming	I have come
I bought	I buy	I will buy	I am buying	I have bought
I slept	I sleep	I will sleep	I am sleeping	I have slept
I knew	I know	I will know	I know	I have known
I fought	I fight	I will fight		
	I think			

F Extension Ideas

Use the library or internet to help you with the following exercise.

1. Write four facts that everyone should know about water safety.

   (a) _____

   (b) _____

   (c) _____

   (d) _____

2. Write four pieces of advice you would give to someone being bullied online or in school.

   (a) _____

   (b) _____

   (c) _____

   (d) _____

G Writing Genre: Recount Writing

You are James Bond and you have just won the cup in the swimming competition.
Write a diary entry of your day at the swimming competition.
Complete the template below.

Title: _____

When did it happen (date)? _____

Setting: _____

Who are the characters in the story?_____

What were they doing? _____

_____

Where did it happen? _____

Why did it happen? _____

_____

Event 1: _____

_____

Event 2: _____

_____

Event 3: _____

_____

Event 4: _____

_____

Afterwards, how did you feel? _____

Now, recount your day.

Dear Diary,

_____

_____

_____

_____

_____
_____
_____
_____
_____
_____
_____
_____
_____
_____
_____
_____
_____
_____
_____
_____
_____
_____
_____
_____
_____
_____
_____
_____
_____

H **Self Reflection**

I was good at: _____

I need to do more work on: _____ Date: _____

A A Little Light Thinking

1. Name the main character in the story. _____

2. What age was Alex? _____

3. What sounds could Alex hear outside the capsule? _____

4. What could Alex see on the aircraft carrier? _____

5. How many divers were there in the water? _____

6. Who developed the memory foam mattress? _____

7. For how long did Cook say that Alex would be unsteady on his feet? _____

8. How many men had met in London to discuss the operation? _____

9. Who or what does the narrator say were back? _____

10. With whom did Alex have a knife fight? _____

B Deeper Thinking

1. Why do you think Alex *would never forget the moment of impact*?

   _____

   _____

2. What do you think is the meaning of the phrase: *Once again his body belonged to him*?

   _____

   _____

3. Why do you think Alex had no physical training before he was sent in the capsule?

   _____

   _____

4. Why do you think there was a floating hospital at sea?

   _____

   _____

5. What questions do you think Cook wanted to ask Alex?

   _____

   _____

6. Why do you think Alex's sleep was troubled?

   _____

   _____

CHALLENGE

Why do you think Kaspar, the eco-terrorist, had tried to kill Alex?

_____

_____

C Vocabulary Work: Wordsearch

Ring the following words in the wordsearch.

a	r	e	k	r	m	a	a	p	c	a	b	l	e	m
c	p	d	y	a	e	h	i	s	p	a	c	e	l	o
h	c	e	e	h	n	t	c	r	u	y	g	r	u	p
a	w	i	n	d	c	i	p	n	c	e	w	k	s	a
o	r	u	r	e	o	y	d	o	i	r	f	y	p	r
t	f	o	u	t	u	a	e	i	c	w	a	y	a	a
i	i	j	o	r	n	t	t	c	i	n	f	c	c	
c	i	m	j	e	t	m	e	a	d	u	l	c	t	h
r	m	o	e	v	e	o	m	r	o	i	k	e	l	u
j	p	d	g	i	r	s	m	e	c	g	v	y	h	t
i	a	u	m	d	e	p	u	p	e	g	b	e	i	e
h	c	l	v	l	d	h	l	o	a	j	b	b	r	i
q	t	e	d	u	g	e	p	h	n	e	y	n	p	t
d	q	n	a	s	t	r	o	n	a	u	t	r	f	q
r	e	v	e	a	l	e	g	q	g	w	e	o	c	v

chaotic ↓ operation ↑
atmosphere ↓ module ↓
impact ↓ capsule ↑
helicopter ↖ winch ↖
cable → parachute ↓
reveal → journey ↑
astronaut → plummeted ↑
diverted ↑ ocean ↓
encountered ↓ aircraft ↘
space → diver ↘

D Working with Sounds: Prefixes un-, uni- and up-

1. **Insert the prefix un-, uni- or up- to make words.**

(a) _____roar	(b) _____cycle	(c) _____lift	(d) _____son	(e) _____fied
(f) _____corn	(g) _____hold	(h) _____true	(i) _____verse	(j) _____bringing
(k) _____able	(l) _____afraid	(m) _____most	(n) _____pleasant	(o) _____usual

2. **Write the words above that are described in the clues.**

   (a) A mythical creature with a single horn: _____

   (b) Another word meaning courageous, daring or brave: _____

   (c) A state of violent and noisy disturbance: _____

   (d) Another word meaning offensive, distasteful or disagreeable: _____

   (e) The name given to the totality of all things in space: _____

   (f) Another word meaning inaccurate, erroneous or false: _____

   (g) To correspond exactly and be in perfect harmony: _____

   (h) Another word meaning loftiest, most elevated or highest: _____

   (i) Another word meaning excite, elate, cheer or boost: _____

   (j) Separate items or parts made into a single unit: _____

   (k) A vehicle that has only one wheel: _____

   (l) Another word meaning ineffectual, helpless or powerless: _____

   (m) Another word meaning out of the ordinary: _____

   (n) Another word meaning rearing or childhood training: _____

   (o) Another word meaning endorse, confirm or defend: _____

17 Down to Earth

E Grammar: Adverbs

> An **adverb** tells us more about a verb. Most adverbs end in **-ly** or **-ily**, e.g. comple**tely**.
> We can make adverbs from adjectives, e.g. steady → stead**ily** / certain → certain**ly**.

Change these adjectives into adverbs and write them in the correct sentences below.

dangerous	accidental	ferocious	extreme	proud
generous	brave	wise	bright	patient
angry	selfish	curious	doubtful	truthful

1. The angry dogs growled loudly and _____ at the intruder.

2. The professor spoke _____ about his knowledge of the space station.

3. The drunken man drove the car _____ down the road.

4. The soldiers fought _____ in the horrible battle during World War I.

5. The teacher spoke _____ to the disruptive and bullying pupil.

6. It was _____ cold in the snow, so I wore my gloves and scarf.

7. The hungry boy waited _____ for his mother to return from the shops.

8. Hercule Poirot looked _____ at the unusual marks on the door.

9. The girl walked _____ onto the stage to receive her prize.

10. The mother looked _____ at her child because the cake had disappeared.

11. The witness spoke _____ about the accident in court.

12. The sun shone _____ in the clear, blue sky during the summer.

13. The young footballer _____ broke the glass in the window.

14. The people in the town contributed _____ to the charity.

15. The bully _____ ate most of the treats at the party.

F Extension Ideas

Use the library or internet to help you with the following exercise.

1. **Write five interesting facts about training to be an astronaut.**

   (a) _____

   (b) _____

   (c) _____

   (d) _____

   (e) _____

2. **Draw the flags of Italy, Spain, Australia and Germany.**

Italy	Spain	Australia	Germany

G **Writing Genre: Recount Writing**

Imagine you are Alex Ryder. Recount what this day in your life might have been be like using the details you read in the story. Complete the template below.

Title: _____

Date: _____

Setting: _____

Who is the story about? _____

When did it happen? _____

Where did it happen? _____

What were they doing? _____

Why did it happen? _____

Event 1: _____

Event 2: _____

Event 3: _____

Event 4: _____

Afterwards, how did you feel? _____

Now, recount your story.

Title: _____

_____

_____

_____

_____

_____

_____

_____

_____

H Self Reflection

I was good at: _____

I need to do more work on: _____ Date: _____

A A Little Light Thinking

1. What is the International Space Station (ISS)?

2. When was the first piece of the ISS, Zarya, carried into space? _____

3. Why was the ISS fully constructed in space and not on Earth?

4. How many missions did it take to completely assemble the ISS in space?_____

5. At, approximately, what speed does the ISS orbit the Earth?_____

6. How many sunsets and sunrises do those on board the ISS experience each day?

7. How many astronauts and cosmonauts in total are on board the ISS at any one time?

8. Describe one method of how electricity is generated on board the ISS.

9. How long does it take an astronaut to train for a mission on board the ISS? _____

10. What tasks do the crew of the ISS carry out daily?

B Deeper Thinking

1. How do you think astronauts return to Earth from the ISS?

2. Why are astronauts required to speak both Russian and English before going on an ISS mission?_____

3. Why do astronauts have to exercise for a minimum of two hours each day on board the ISS?

4. What do you think is the biggest challenge for astronauts living in space?

5. In what way do astronauts get a clearer view of the sun, stars and other galaxies from the ISS? _____

6. Why do you think disinfectant wipes are used for cleaning on the ISS?

CHALLENGE

How do you think the experiments conducted on board the ISS are of benefit to people living on Earth?

18 The International Space Station

C Working with Sounds: Suffixes -cy and -ist

The suffix -cy is added to words to form nouns that show a condition or the state of something. For words ending in te, we drop the te and add -cy, e.g. pirate → piracy / numerate → numeracy.
The suffix -ist is added to words to form nouns meaning a person who practises or is concerned with something. With most words we simply add -ist, e.g. motorist / harpist.
If the word ends in e or y, drop the e or y and add -ist, e.g. type → typist / colony → colonist.

Write the correct -cy or -ist ending for the following words.

(a) private: _____
(b) novel: _____
(c) type: _____
(d) delicate: _____
(e) solo: _____
(f) final: _____
(g) guitar: _____
(h) pirate: _____
(i) accurate: _____
(j) numerate: _____
(k) botany: _____
(l) harp: _____
(m) candidate: _____
(n) mediate: _____
(o) tour: _____
(p) violin: _____
(q) supreme: _____
(r) colony: _____

D Comprehension Work: Cloze Procedure

Use the words in the word box to complete the story below.

seen	healthy	biggest	speed	inside
above	piece	bright	inhabited	zero
minimum	unmanned	laboratory	build	launched
crew	lasts	adapt	upset	conduct

The International Space Station

The International Space Station (ISS) is an orbiting _____. It is the _____ and heaviest object ever flown in space. It travels around the Earth at an average _____ of 800 km/h. It flies around 400 km _____ the Earth. 16 countries, including the USA, Russia, Japan, France, Brazil, and Canada worked together to _____ the station. The ISS was built piece by _____. Zarya was the first piece of the ISS _____ into space in 1998. The station was _____ until November 2000. It has been _____ every day since then. The station can carry up to six _____ members.

Each ISS mission usually _____ about six months. Crew members have to exercise for a _____ of two hours each day to stay fit and keep their bones and muscles strong and _____. The human body has to _____ to the abnormal environment of space. Some astronauts feel dizzy and may have an _____ stomach during the first few days of a space flight while they get used to _____ gravity. Astronauts _____ many different experiments both _____ and outside the space laboratory. The ISS can be _____ from nearly every place on Earth at some point in time. It appears as a _____, slow-moving, white dot in the night sky.

E Grammar: Prepositions

Prepositions are words that indicate direction, position, time, or location, e.g. about, before.

1. **Insert the most appropriate preposition from the word box in the following.**

across	until	during	over	into	among
below	between	near	underneath	around	before

(a) Zarya was the first piece of the ISS carried _____ space.

(b) The football manager paced nervously _____ the chaning room while giving his speech.

(c) The employees take two breaks _____ their working day.

(d) Weeds began to grow _____ the beautiful beds of roses in the garden.

(e) The referee ran _____ the pitch to give a yellow card to the rough player.

(f) We are all advised to think carefully _____ we leap into anything.

(g) The boxer was disqualified for hitting his opponent _____ the belt.

(h) The tennis umpire sat in his chair _____ the game ended.

(i) They parked their car at the fountain _____ the concert venue.

(j) In the nursery rhyme, it is said that the cow jumped _____ the moon.

(k) The family had a picnic _____ a towering oak tree.

(l) Cian stood in the queue _____ his friends Bobby and Cathy.

2. **Put each of the following prepositions into sentences of your own below.**

(a) beneath: _____

(b) against: _____

(c) beside: _____

(d) through: _____

(e) across: _____

(f) between: _____

(g) inside: _____

(h) around: _____

(i) ahead of: _____

(j) next to: _____

F Extension Ideas

Use the library or internet to help you with the following exercise.

Write four interesting facts about the International Space Station.

(a) _____

(b) _____

(c) _____

(d) _____

G **Writing Genre: Report Writing**

Research, plan and write a report on the first ISS Mission (November 2000–March 2001).
Complete the template below.

Title: **The First ISS Mission**

What was the name of the craft?_____

From where did it launch? _____

Who was on board? _____

To where was it going? _____

When did it land? _____

Interesting facts: _____

_____

Summarising comment: _____

_____

Now, write your report.

Title: **The First ISS Mission**

_____

_____

_____

_____

_____

_____

_____

_____

_____

_____

H **Self Reflection**

I was good at: _____

I need to do more work on: _____ Date: _____

A A Little Light Thinking

1. Describe what the streets in the town used to be like. _____
    _____

2. What was Felix's plan? _____
    _____

3. What type of clothes was Felix wearing? _____

4. Where does Felix think his parents are? _____

5. What were Mr and Mrs Radzyn's occupations when Felix lived on the street?
    _____

6. Where did Felix hide? _____

7. For what country did Felix's parents hope to get visas? _____

8. What game were the two little kids playing in the street? _____

B Deeper Thinking

1. How do you think Felix ended up living in an orphanage?
    _____

2. Why do you think he keeps dreaming of food shops when he is in the orphanage?
    _____

3. Why do you think the whole street is deserted? _____
    _____

4. How does Felix feel when he finds that there are no books in the shop? Why?
    _____

5. Why do you think the Radzyn family have moved into Felix's home?
    _____

6. To whom do you think Mr Radzyn wanted to hand Felix over?
    _____

7. Why do you think Felix starts to panic when he hears what the little girl says?
    _____

8. Describe Felix's character traits. _____
    _____

CHALLENGE

Felix is optimistic about meeting his parents again. Do you think he will meet them again? Give reasons for your answer.

_____
_____

C Vocabulary Work: Crossword

Complete the crossword using the clues below.

ACROSS

1. People whose traditional religion is Judaism
5. The capital of this country is Washington DC
7. A place empty of people
8. A chewy, black sweet
11. To identify someone
18. Knowledge/skill acquired over time
20. A home for the care of orphans

DOWN

2. An opening/door
3. Not alike in any way
4. A permit to enter a country
6. A person who buys goods from a shop
9. A sudden, uncontrollable fear
10. A crash or a disaster
12. Small stones in a street
13. A road with shops/houses
14. Wearing no shoes or socks
15. To give an answer
16. An orange coloured vegetable
17. The writer of a book
19. Trees grow here

D Working with Sounds: Suffixes -able and -ible

The suffixes -able and -ible usually mean *capable of being*, e.g. enjoyable, possible, etc.
When the first part of the word is a root word, we usually add -able, e.g. comfortable.
When the first part is not a root word, we add -ible, e.g. horrible, visible.

1. **Ring the correct spelling of each word below.**

   (a) impossible / impossable (b) terrible / terrable (c) adorible / adorable

   (d) payible / payable (e) compatable / compatible (f) flexible / flexable

   (g) noticeable / noticible (h) reversable / reversible (i) eligable / eligible

   (j) acceptible / acceptable (k) invincible / invincable (l) sensable / sensible

2. **Write the dictionary meaning of the first six words above.**

   (a) _____

   (b) _____

   (c) _____

   (d) _____

   (e) _____

   (f) _____

E Grammar: Conjunctions

A **conjunction** joins words, phrases or sentences together, e.g. The street is narrow like I remember **and** the buildings are all two levels high.

1. Choose the most suitable conjunction from the list for each sentence below.

before	when	but	because	until
or	since	and	although	so

(a) 'Would you like a chocolate biscuit _____ would you prefer a plain one?' I asked Natasha at the party.

(b) I am not allowed out to play _____ I complete my homework.

(c) Mum went to the dentist _____ she had a terrible toothache.

(d) 'I'll be really happy _____ my mother comes home,' said Danny.

(e) 'It's been a long time _____ I played chess but I will try to play,' he said.

(f) 'I don't like dogs _____ I absolutely love cats,' said Sofia.

(g) 'It is wet, _____ you would be sensible to bring an umbrella,' advised Mum.

(h) I like to eat sausages, eggs _____ bacon rashers for my breakfast.

(i) Jack always brushes his teeth _____ he goes to bed, which is good.

(j) Orla is the best player on the team _____ she is the smallest.

2. Write sentences using the following conjunctions.

(a) and: _____

(b) but: _____

(c) because: _____

(d) so: _____

(e) if: _____

F Extension Ideas

Use the library or internet to help you with the following exercise.

1. Write five interesting facts about Anne Frank.

(a) _____

(b) _____

(c) _____

(d) _____

(e) _____

2. Write five interesting facts about *Kristallnacht*.

(a) _____

(b) _____

(c) _____

(d) _____

(e) _____

G **Writing Genre: Report Writing**

Felix dreamed about his home and his town when he was in the orphanage.
Write a report titled: *My Special Place.* Complete the template below.

Title: **My Special Place**

What did he see? _____

Where did he see it? _____

Description 1: What did Felix's home look like? _____

Description 2: What did Felix's town look like? _____

Where was he going? _____

Who was with him? _____

When did this happen? _____

Summarising comment: _____

_____

Now, write your report.

Title: **My Special Place**

_____

_____

_____

_____

_____

_____

_____

_____

_____

_____

_____

_____

_____

_____

H Self Reflection

I was good at: _____

I need to do more work on: _____ Date: _____

A A Little Light Thinking

1. What happened to the newcomer when he fell asleep?

   _____

2. How did David know how old he was?_____

3. How did David feel about the man?_____

4. What did the man strike? _____

5. How long did David wait before he climbed the barbed wire?

   _____

6. Why did he start walking when he got to the other side of the fence?

   _____

7. What did David imagine was inside the cloth bundle?

   _____

8. When would the search party be sent out after David?

   _____

B Deeper Thinking

1. Why do you think David does not use the man's first name?

   _____

2. What would you have done if you were David? Explain.

   _____

   _____

3. Why did he feel that his escape had taken a long time even though it had only taken
   a few minutes?_____

   _____

4. Why do you think David was shivering with the cold even though it wasn't cold at all?

   _____

   _____

5. Why might David have had a burning desire to get the better of the man?

   _____

6. Why do you think that the contents of the bundle were so important to David?

   _____

CHALLENGE

How is this story similar to the story you read from *The Hunger Games*?

_____

_____

20 I Am David

C Vocabulary Work: Thesaurus Work

1. Ring the word that is closest in meaning to the original word.

muttering:	(a) shouting	(b) whispering	(c) screaming	(d) roaring
trap:	(a) release	(b) liberate	(c) trick	(d) escape
several:	(a) none	(b) few	(c) one	(d) many
appeared:	(a) vanished	(b) emerged	(c) one	(d) departed
triumph:	(a) victory	(b) disaster	(c) loss	(d) ticket
dangerous:	(a) knife	(b) harmless	(c) risky	(d) safe
shivering:	(a) trembling	(b) calm	(c) serene	(d) composed
thicket:	(a) garden	(b) tree	(c) clearing	(d) wood
undecided:	(a) doubtful	(b) certain	(c) sure	(d) definite
angrily:	(a) happily	(b) calmly	(c) furiously	(d) serenely
victory:	(a) downfall	(b) win	(c) defea	(d) loss
amusing:	(a) humorous	(b) boring	(c) depressing	(d) tiring
respond:	(a) overlook	(b) ignore	(c) peace	(d) answer
quickly:	(a) slowly	(b) leisurely	(c) gradually	(d) rapidly
whirl:	(a) calm	(b) spin	(c) tranquil	(d) stop

2. Write the following words in short sentences to show their meanings.

(a) fainter: _____

(b) grating: _____

(c) bundle: _____

(d) struggled: _____

(e) respond: _____

(f) accustomed: _____

D Working with Sounds: Suffixes **-less, -ness** and **-ment**

The suffix **-less** means **without**, e.g. David saw before him the endless succession of days.
The suffix **-ness** means **has** or **being**, e.g. David's eyes became accustomed to the darkness.
The suffix **-ment** means **action** or **result**, e.g. There wasn't much enjoyment in the camp.

1. Write the suffix -less, -ness or -ment to make new words.

flavour____	amaze____	fit____	manage____	sleep____
hope____	wire____	amuse____	commit____	achieve____
abandon____	playful____	senti____	harm____	reck____
forgive____	bitter____	clever____	still____	bottom____
achieve____	bald____	heart____	price____	kind____
dry____	engage____	encourage____	happi____	weight____

2. Write eight more words ending with -less, -ness or -ment.

(a) _____ (b) _____ (c) _____ (d) _____

(e) _____ (f) _____ (g) _____ (h) _____

E Grammar: Abbreviations

An **abbreviation** is a shortened word, created by omitting a number of letters in that word, e.g. lane → ln. / adjective → adj. If the last letter of the abbreviation is the same as the last letter of the word itself, we don't use a full stop at the end, e.g. Doctor → Dr

1. Write the full word/phrase for each of the following abbreviations

   (a) TD _____   (b) PC _____

   (c) MP _____   (d) Gen. _____

   (e) DOB _____   (f) FF _____

   (g) FG _____   (h) Lab. _____

2. Write the following using capital letters and punctuation marks. Abbreviate each underlined word.

   (a) <u>miss</u> kate matthews: _____

   (b) adelaide <u>road</u>: _____

   (c) dublin <u>street</u>: _____

   (d) <u>monday</u>, 12th july 2019: _____

   (e) <u>mister</u> murphy: _____

   (f) <u>professor</u> john farrell: _____

3. Write the names of 10 Irish counties with their abbreviation beside each one.

   (a) _____   (b) _____

   (c) _____   (d) _____

   (e) _____   (f) _____

   (g) _____   (h) _____

   (i) _____   (j) _____

F Extension Ideas

Use the library or internet to help you with the following exercise.

1. Write six interesting facts about an attempted escape from the prison on Alcatraz Island in San Francisco Bay, California, USA.

   (a) _____

   (b) _____

   (c) _____

   (d) _____

   (e) _____

   (f) _____

2. Write two reasons why people might have to flee from their own country.

   (a) _____

   (b) _____

G **Writing Genre: Persuasive Writing**

The guards in the concentration camp wear uniforms. Write a persuasive argument for the following statement: *The guards in the concentration camp should not wear uniforms.* Complete the template below.

Title: **The Guards in the Concentration Camp Should Not Wear Uniforms**

Introduction: Write a statement giving your opinion.

_____

Reason 1: _____

_____

Reason 2: _____

_____

Reason 3: _____

_____

Conclusion: Give a summary of your main points. _____

_____

Finally, I think that I have shown… _____

_____

_____

Now, write your persuasive argument.

Title: **The Guards in the Concentration Camp Should Not Wear Uniforms**

_____

_____

_____

_____

_____

_____

_____

_____

_____

_____

_____

_____

_____

_____

_____

_____

_____

_____

_____

_____

_____

_____

_____

_____

_____

_____

_____

_____

_____

_____

H **Self Reflection**

I was good at: _____

I need to do more work on: _____ Date: _____

21 World War II

A A Little Light Thinking

1. For how many years did World War II last? _____

2. Who was the leader of Germany during World War II? _____

3. What is the meaning of the word *blitzkrieg*? _____

   _____

4. Where did Londoners hide when bombs were dropped on their city?

   _____

5. On what date did D-Day occur? _____

6. What was the name of the Russian army? _____

7. What was the *Master Race* also known as? _____

   _____

8. What do the letters UN stand for? _____

9. Approximately, how many Russians died because of World War II?

   _____

10. On what date did the USA drop atomic bombs on Japan? _____

B Deeper Thinking

1. Why do you think Ireland stayed neutral during World War II?

   _____

2. Why do you think Britain and France declared war when Germany invaded Poland?

   _____

3. Why do you think the Japanese bombed Pearl Harbour in Hawaii?

   _____

   _____

4. What difficulties might the Allied Forces have faced when landing on the
   beaches in Normandy? _____

   _____

5. Why do you think Italy changed sides during the war?

   _____

   _____

6. Was setting up the UN important? Give two reasons for your answer.

   (a) _____

   (b) _____

CHALLENGE

Do you think a world war could happen again? Give two reasons.

(a) _____

(b) _____

C Vocabulary Work: Synonyms

Remember: Synonyms are words similar or close to similar in meaning, e.g. ill → sick.

Write the word closest in meaning to the underlined word in each sentence.

trespassers	impartial	feeble	eradicate
defeated	succumbed	control	plan

1. Ireland was one of very few countries in the world to remain <u>neutral</u>. _____
2. The Germans used a <u>tactic</u> called *blitzkrieg*. _____
3. France <u>surrendered</u> to Germany very early on in the war. _____
4. Germany had <u>conquered</u> almost all of Europe. _____
5. Anti-aircraft guns would try to shoot down the <u>invaders</u>. _____
6. Ships and boats were used to transport the soldiers to Normandy in an attempt to free France from German <u>occupation</u>. _____
7. Hitler's final solution was to <u>exterminate</u> all of the Jewish people. _____
8. The old, disabled and <u>weak</u> were gassed and buried in mass graves. _____

D Comprehension Work: Cloze Procedure

Use the words in the word box to complete the story below.

invaded	surrendered	Germany	six	Adolf
tactic	Axis	occupying	wave	attacked
naval	London	begun	stations	Hawaii
shelters	Europe	Britain	declared	Roosevelt

World War II

World War II lasted for almost _____ years. It was a war between the Allies and the Axis Powers. On the side of the Allies were 50 countries, including _____, France, the USA and Russia. They fought against the _____ Powers, which was a group of nine countries that included _____, Japan and Italy.

The German leader, _____ Hitler, wanted to create a new empire. When he _____ Poland in 1939, Britain and France _____ war on Germany. World War II had _____.

The Germans used a _____ called *blitzkrieg*, which involved surprising their enemies and _____ their lands before they could organise themselves. During the *Blitz* in _____, German aeroplanes dropped _____ after wave of bombs. People would rush to air-raid _____ or London Underground train _____. By the summer of 1941, Germany had conquered almost all of _____.

In December 1941, the Japanese bombed an American _____ base in Pearl Harbour in _____. More than 2,000 Americans lost their lives. President _____ declared war on Japan the following day.

The Allies began to fight back after D-Day and Germany was now being _____ from all sides. Germany _____ in May 1945 and Adolf Hitler was found dead in an underground bunker shortly afterwards.

E Working with Words: Occupations

Ring the occupations hidden in the wordsearch below.

a	z	a	t	a	b	x	x	m	a	u	v
j	b	r	e	e	u	r	f	i	t	s	h
j	m	t	y	t	t	o	l	y	a	a	a
o	g	i	w	s	c	t	o	i	e	i	i
o	k	s	a	i	h	c	l	r	a	r	r
a	b	t	l	t	e	o	i	o	e	t	d
y	y	b	r	n	r	d	s	y	h	s	r
t	s	i	r	o	l	f	w	i	e	i	e
k	o	l	d	d	w	a	d	a	r	t	s
c	s	i	l	i	l	h	e	s	u	n	s
r	e	t	n	e	p	r	a	c	v	e	e
a	h	t	e	a	c	h	e	r	w	d	r

artist ↓ florist ←
butcher ↓ hairdresser ↓
carpenter ← sailor ↙
doctor ↑ dentist ↑
teacher → lawyer ↗

F Grammar: Initialisms and Acronyms

An **initialism** is an abbreviation consisting of initial letters pronounced separately, e.g. the UN → the United Nations / AIB → Allied Irish Bank.
An **acronym** is an abbreviation consisting of initial letters pronounced as a new word, e.g. SWAT → Special Weapons And Tactics.

1. **Match the initialisms to their meanings.**

ATM ●	● Compact Disc
BBC ●	● Digital Versatile Disc
EU ●	● Automated Teller Machine
DVD ●	● Common Agricultural Policy
FBI ●	● British Broadcasting Corporation
UFO ●	● European Union
CD ●	● Unidentified Flying Object
CAP ●	● Federal Bureau of Investigation

BLT ●	● Greenwich Mean Time
ASAP ●	● Thank God It's Friday
TGIF ●	● Save Our Souls
NBA ●	● Bacon, Lettuce, Tomato
FYI ●	● As Soon As Possible
PR ●	● For Your Information
SOS ●	● National Basketball Association
GMT ●	● Public Relations

2. **Match the acronyms to their meanings.**

GIF ●	● Also Known As
AWOL ●	● Read-Only Memory
VAT ●	● Graphics Interchange Format
AKA ●	● Value Added Tax
ROM ●	● Absent Without Leave

SWAT ●	● Laugh Out Loud
POW ●	● Special Weapons And Tactics
RAM ●	● Personal Identification Number
LOL ●	● Prisoner Of War
PIN ●	● Random Access Memory

G Extension Ideas

Use the library or internet to help you with the following exercise.

1. **Write the names of four other countries that fought on the side of the Allies.**

   (a) _____ (b) _____ (c) _____ (d) _____

2. **Write two interesting facts about the concentration camps.**

   (a) _____

   (b) _____

H **Writing Genre: Persuasive Writing**

Plan and write a persuasive argument convincing your friends that the
USA was right to enter World War II in December 1941.
Complete the template below.

Title: **The USA was right to enter World War II in December 1941**

State your point of view: _____

_____

Reason 1: My first reason is _____

_____

Reason 2: A further reason is _____

_____

Reason 3: Furthermore, _____

_____

Conclusion: Some people might argue that _____

_____

Finally, I think that I have shown... _____

_____

Now, write your persuasive argument.

Title: **The USA was right to enter World War II in December 1941**

_____

_____

_____

_____

_____

_____

_____

_____

Self Reflection

I was good at: _____

I need to do more work on: _____ Date: _____

A A Little Light Thinking

1. What did Helix say were the only things on the Lesser Islands?

2. What did Helix say would hide their boat?

3. Why did he not want to know the names of the children?

4. Who was Seagrape?

5. What lay beneath the majestic trees?

6. How many jaguars could the children see?

7. What were sweeper vines?

8. What could Maya see through the trees?

9. How old was Penny?

10. Why did Helix advise the children not to move suddenly?

B Deeper Thinking

1. Why do you think Helix had the bow and arrows with him?

2. Why do you think Maya didn't want to leave their boat?

3. What reasons did Simon have for being in awe of Helix?

4. How do we know that the area with the trees looked eerie?

5. What do you think made Penny so scared when she woke up?

6. How do we know the jaguar was sleepy when it woke up?

CHALLENGE

What do you think the children should do next?

C Vocabulary Work: Thesaurus Work

1. **Write the words from the story similar in meaning to the following word groups.**

   (a) sheer, elevated, hilly, raised: s_____

   (b) intruder, guest, outsider, newcomer: s_____

   (c) glistening, gleaming, dazzling, shimmering: g_____

   (d) disguise, cover, cloak, conceal: c_____

   (e) speedily, hastily, hurriedly, rapidly: q_____

   (f) chat, discussion, speech, talk: c_____

   (g) huge, massive, large, colossal: g_____

   (h) sleeping, dozing, resting, snoozing: n_____

   (i) cry, bawl, howl, sob: w_____

   (j) scared, terrified, frightened, startled: p_____

2. **Write four thesaurus words for each of the following words from the story.**

   (a) danger: _____

   (b) descended: _____

   (c) amazement: _____

   (d) beneath: _____

   (e) magnificent: _____

D Working with Sounds: Suffixes -th and -ht

It can be difficult to know if a word ends in **-th** or **-ht**. Here are some hints:
(a) The ending **-th** has a softer sound, e.g. brea**th**, whereas **-ht** sounds like **t**, e.g. lig**ht**.
(b) If the third last letter is a **g**, this is usually followed by **-ht**. Exceptions include len**g**th, stren**g**th where the **g** is not silent. Otherwise, the word ends with **-th**.

Ring the -th and -ht words in the wordsearch.

z	y	g	b	n	h	n	z	u	j	t	e
v	h	t	u	r	t	s	h	n	p	g	y
b	o	b	r	e	a	t	h	d	e	n	e
s	r	o	d	y	e	o	m	e	z	k	s
a	i	o	v	t	n	u	j	r	l	q	i
f	g	g	u	h	e	j	f	g	w	h	g
v	h	q	d	g	b	k	d	r	l	t	h
g	t	f	a	i	h	u	j	o	i	r	t
m	b	l	n	n	z	t	t	w	y	a	y
f	t	s	m	d	o	t	j	t	d	e	q
z	x	l	f	i	f	g	s	h	b	f	r
l	x	z	d	m	l	i	g	h	t	v	o

right ↓   beneath ↑

truth ←   light →

breath →   midnight ↑

undergrowth ↓   eyesight ↓

brought ↘   earth ↑

E **Grammar: I and Me**

The **personal pronouns** **I** and **me** are often used incorrectly.
(a) Use the pronoun **I** along with other subjective pronouns **we**, **he**, **she**, **you**, and **they** when the pronoun is the subject of a verb, e.g. Helix and **I** can take you there.
(b) Use the pronoun **me** along with other **objective pronouns** such as **us**, **him**, **her**, **you**, and **them** when the pronoun is the object of a preposition, e.g. You'd better stick with **me**.

1. **Complete the following using the correct word (I or me) in each sentence.**

(a) Jane and _____ are going for coffee in town this afternoon.

(b) Peter spent the day with _____ before going back home.

(c) The dog followed _____ to the end of the road before turning back.

(d) Mum took Stephen and _____ to the shop to buy bread.

(e) She told John and _____ to get ready to go to the concert.

(f) 'You and _____ need to get moving or we will be late,' said Amelia.

(g) He needs to talk to Joe or _____ urgently.

(h) 'If Jane and _____ are late, we will eat dinner later,' said Dave.

(i) 'This discussion is between you and _____, so don't repeat it,' said Pat.

(j) She told him and _____ the truth eventually, before her mother arrived.

2. **Ring the correct pronoun (I or me) for each sentence. Write them.**

(a) Who will be attending with Tom and _____?   I / me

(b) He wants to give presents to Susan and _____.   I / me

(c) The old lady and _____ were sitting on the bus.   I / me

(d) Kevin, Lisa, Cora and _____ are going to the cinema.   I / me

(e) You can leave the rest of the sweets with Liam and _____.   I / me

(f) She doesn't want to be seen with my father or _____.   I / me

(g) Both my friend Sarah and _____ would like to visit the park.   I / me

(h) She really wanted to come travelling with Kim and _____.   I / me

(i) My sister and _____ wanted to go camping in the forest.   I / me

(j) Jason, George and _____ all wanted to finish our homework early. I / me

F **Extension Ideas**

Use the library or internet to help you with the following exercise.

1. **Name eight islands in Europe.**

(a) _____   (b) _____

(c) _____   (d) _____

(e) _____   (f) _____

(g) _____   (h) _____

2. **Write three interesting facts about one of the islands above.**

(a) _____

(b) _____

(c) _____

G **Writing Genre: Procedural Writing**

The children will have to find shelter on the island before it gets dark.
Write a step-by-step list of instructions on how to build a shelter for the night.
Complete the step-by-step procedure below.

Procedure 1

Title: **How to Build a Shelter for the Night**

Aim: What do you want to do? _____

_____

Requirements (equipment needed): _____

_____

Method: Step-by-step instructions

Step 1: _____

_____

Step 2: _____

_____

Step 3: _____

_____

Step 4: _____

_____

Step 5: _____

_____

Step 6: _____

_____

Step 7: _____

_____

Did you achieve your goal? _____

_____

Procedure 2

Title: **How to Survive in the Wild**

Aim: What do you want to do? _____

_____

Requirements (equipment needed): _____

_____

Method: Step-by-step instructions

Step 1: _____

_____

Step 2: _____

_____

Step 3: _____

_____

Step 4: _____

_____

Step 5: _____

_____

Step 6: _____

_____

Step 7: _____

_____

Did you achieve your goal? _____

_____

H **Self Reflection**

I was good at: _____

I need to do more work on: _____ Date: _____

23 The Wolf Wilder

A A Little Light Thinking

1. Who did the drivers expect to come and untie the wolf? _____

2. What colour was the wolf's fur? _____

3. Why did Feo check inside the wolf's mouth?

   _____

4. How was Marina's hair when she emerged from the house?

   _____

5. What did the new wolf do in the wardrobe of the countess?

   _____

6. What was stuck between the wolf's teeth? _____

7. What did Feo think they should call the new wolf? _____

8. What colour was the ointment that Marina rubbed on the wolf's paw? _____

B Deeper Thinking

1. How do we know that Feo was very strong?

   _____

   _____

2. Why do you think Feo asked the driver if he had passed any soldiers on the way?

   _____

   _____

3. How do we know that the wolf wasn't well looked after before coming to Feo?

   _____

   _____

4. Do you think Feo got on well with new people? Explain.

   _____

   _____

5. How do we know from the story that wolves are dangerous creatures?

   _____

   _____

6. Why do you think Marina told Feo to pack a bag and keep it by the back door?

   _____

   _____

CHALLENGE

(a) **What do you think is meant by the word *lapushka*?**

(b) **Do we have any word in the Irish language that would be close
    in meaning to *lapushka*?**

(a) _____

(b) _____

C Vocabulary Work: Jumbled letters

Use the clues to unscramble the words from the story. Write them.

1. An officer in the army: (nergeal) _____
2. The separate compartments of a train: (rraicgsea) _____
3. Can't be seen: (vinsbliie) _____
4. A precious metal: (vislre) _____
5. Growth of hair on the face: (dbrae) _____
6. A word meaning to rot: (ycdea) _____
7. To have fallen down and become unconscious: (lapcodels) _____
8. An opening into the nose: (rtlisno) _____
9. The trunk of the body: (ootrs) _____
10. A place to store clothes: (drwbreoa) _____
11. A soft, silky piece of fabric: (levvte) _____
12. Easily broken or damaged: (glfarie) _____
13. A healing lotion or cream: (menoittn) _____
14. A small church: (plchae) _____
15. The feminine word for wizards: (wchties) _____

D Working with Sounds: Suffixes -ful and -ward

The **suffix -ful** means *to be full of*, e.g. beautiful → to be full of beauty.
The **suffix -ward** or **wards** means *indicating direction*, e.g. toward / towards.

Add -ful or -ward(s) to the following and put them in the correct sentences below.

back_____	grate_____	forget_____	care_____	home_____
straightfor_____	colour_____	for_____	truth_____	in_____

1. The nails on the lion's paw curled _____, causing it great pain.
2. The lady sewed the _____ blanket to put on the child's bed.
3. The instructions were very _____, so I played the game immediately.
4. The charity was _____ for all of the donations it received.
5. The cat crept _____ silently and pounced on the unsuspecting mouse.
6. I was _____ not to bang my head as I crawled under the gate.
7. She gave a _____ glance at the people before exiting the room.
8. My grandmother says she gets _____ sometimes when she is tired.
9. On his _____ journey he met hazardous conditions on the icy roads.
10. The _____ man gave an honest, eyewitness account of the crime.

23 The Wolf Wilder

E **Grammar: Concord Between Nouns and Verbs**

> **Concord** is the agreement between words in **gender**, **number**, **case** and **person**.
> (a)   If the subject of a sentence is singular, the verb must be singular.
> (b)   If the subject is plural, the verb must be plural, e.g. **She** (subject) **is** (verb) going to town. **They** (subject) **are** (verb) not like dogs.
> (c)   **Collective nouns** are used in the singular form, e.g. The **team is** in training.

1.   **Use is or are in the sentences below.**

   (a)   The pages of the book _____ held together by a paper clip.

   (b)   The note stated that he _____ going to the cinema tomorrow night.

   (c)   The box of chocolates _____ for the whole class to share.

   (d)   The children _____ listening carefully to their teacher today.

   (e)   A plumber and an electrician _____ needed to install the washing machine.

   (f)   The teacher and the students _____ going on a tour to Dublin Zoo.

   (g)   Mary or Susan _____ in charge of the office when the boss is at the meeting.

   (h)   There _____ some breadcrumbs lying on the floor.

   (i)   No one _____ allowed in the playground today because it is too wet.

   (j)   40 km _____ a long distance for anyone to run.

2.   **Use was or were in the sentences below.**

   (a)   The children _____ free from school due to the heavy snow.

   (b)   The team _____ training very hard for the big game on the weekend.

   (c)   The chocolates in the box _____ melting in the sun.

   (d)   The army _____ on manoeuvres for the whole day.

   (e)   The members of the army unit _____ all shattered after the difficult manoeuvres.

   (f)   The crew members _____ all highly skilled and well trained.

   (g)   The bouquet of flowers _____ presented to the lady in the canteen.

   (h)   The flowers _____ all wilted when the lady arrived home.

   (i)   The government _____ debating the merits of the law change in the chamber.

   (j)   The members of the government _____ sitting in the chamber.

F **Extension Ideas**

Use the library or internet to help you with the following exercise.

1.   **Write six places inhabited by wild wolves.**

   (a) _____   (b) _____   (c) _____

   (d) _____   (e) _____   (f) _____

2.   **Name four species of wolf.**

   (a) _____

   (b) _____

   (c) _____

   (d) _____

G Writing Genre: Procedural Writing

Feo and her mother are wolf wilders. They take excellent care of the wolves in their care.
Write a step-by-step set of instructions for taking care of a pet.
Complete the step-by-step procedure below.

Procedure 1

Title: **Taking Care of a Pet**

Aim: What do you want to do? _____

Requirements (equipment needed): _____

_____

Method: Step-by-step instructions

Step 1: _____

_____

Step 2: _____

_____

Step 3: _____

_____

Step 4: _____

_____

Step 5: _____

_____

Step 6: _____

_____

Step 7: _____

_____

Did you achieve your goal? _____

_____

Procedure 2

Title: **Taking Care of My Teeth**

Aim: What do you want to do? _____

Requirements (equipment needed): _____

_____

Method: Step-by-step instructions

Step 1: _____

_____

Step 2: _____

_____

Step 3: _____

_____

Step 4: _____

_____

Step 5: _____

_____

Step 6: _____

_____

Step 7: _____

_____

Did you achieve your goal? _____

_____

H **Self Reflection**

I was good at: _____

I need to do more work on: _____ Date: _____

A A Little Light Thinking

1. Name the three Oceans that border Russia.

    (a) _____ (b) _____ (c) _____

2. Explain the meaning of the word *permafrost*.

    _____

3. How many kilometres in length is the River Volga? _____

4. What is the most famous attraction in the city of St Petersburg?

    _____

5. What is the approximate population of Russia? _____

6. Name four domestic animals raised by farmers in Russia.

    (a) _____ (b) _____

    (c) _____ (d) _____

7. Name four sports that people enjoy in Russia.

    (a) _____ (b) _____

    (c) _____ (d) _____

8. What is the name of the popular souvenir made up of nesting dolls? _____

B Deeper Thinking

1. Why do you think trees don't grow in the tundra?

    _____

2. Why do you think the Kremlin is enclosed by high walls?

    _____

3. Why do you think the steppes were once home to the Cossack horsemen?

    _____

4. Give two reasons why you think the majority of Russians live in cities and towns.

    (a) _____

    (b) _____

5. Write two reasons why tourists might want to visit Russia on holidays.

    (a) _____

    (b) _____

6. Why do you think Russians are interested in space travel and exploration?

    _____

CHALLENGE

What modes of transport do you think are most popular in Russia? Explain.

(a) _____

(b) _____

C Vocabulary Work: True or False?

Write true or false after each statement.

1. Russia has a population of approximately 144 million. _____
2. *Taiga* is a Russian word meaning *treeless heights*. _____
3. The tundra is covered with snow all year round. _____
4. Russia is divided by the Ural Mountains. _____
5. The majority of Russia's oil reserves are found in Siberia. _____
6. The Inuit tribe lives in the Kremlin. _____
7. St Petersburg is the capital city of Russia. _____
8. The River Volga is the longest river in Europe. _____
9. *Nerpa* are mammals that live in Lake Baikal. _____
10. *Borscht* is a Russian pie made for special occasions. _____
11. The first jewelled Fabergé egg was known as *Hen Egg*. _____
12. The first human being to orbit the Earth was Yuri Gargarin. _____
13. Tourists can travel throughout Russia on the Trans-Moscow Railway. _____
14. The most famous attraction in Moscow is the Winter Palace. _____
15. The largest city in the east of Russia is Vladivostok. _____

D Comprehension Work: Cloze Procedure

Use the words in the word box to complete the story below.

Pacific	vast	largest	sturgeon	Baikal	Bolshoi	two
Volga	Caspian	Ural	Moscow	tourists	caviar	population
longest	Siberia	weather	Trans-Siberian	world	expensive	

Russia

Russia is the _____ country in the world. It crosses _____ continents and borders three oceans. It covers a vast area extending from the Baltic Sea in the west to the _____ Ocean in the east, and from the Arctic in the north to the _____ Sea in the South. Russia is so _____ that its territory crosses 11 time zones.

In parts of Russia such as the Black Sea, the _____ is warm throughout the year. In other parts, such as _____, the weather is dry and extremely cold. The _____ Mountain range divides Russia geographically. The River _____ in western Russia, is the _____ river in Europe. Half of Russia's _____ lives within its river basin.

The number of _____ visiting Russia has grown dramatically over the last number of years. The capital of Russia, _____, is famous for Red Square, the Kremlin buildings and Lenin's Mausoleum. The _____, which is the most famous classical ballet company in the world, is also located in Moscow.

The _____ Railway carries freight and passengers across Russia. It passes Lake _____, the deepest lake in the _____. The Caspian Sea is famous for its _____ fish, whose roe is processed into _____, a famous delicacy and one of the world's most _____ foods.

E Grammar: Colons and Semi-colons

A **colon** can be used:
(a) To introduce **a list of items** after a complete, independent sentence, e.g.
Four countries bordering Russia are: Norway, China, Poland and Latvia.
(b) After words such as **example** and **remember**, e.g.
Remember: Always brush your teeth after every meal.
(c) To introduce the **spoken words** of somebody, e.g.
Oscar Wilde said: 'No man is rich enough to buy back his past.'

A **semi-colon** can be used:
(a) To join two complete sentences that are closely related to one another
by eliminating the conjunction, e.g. They love ballet; I can't stand it.
(b) To join two separate sentences with words such as **however**, **consequently**, **therefore**,
moreover, **otherwise**, etc. e.g. He was advised to stop smoking; otherwise, he would die.

Rewrite the following sentences inserting a colon or semi-colon in each case.

1. His jobs for the day were the washing, the vacuuming and the dusting.

2. We went to see the ballet *Swan Lake* it was my mother's birthday.

3. Here are his favourite pastimes golf, soccer, reading and tennis.

4. Remember it is necessary to stop at a red light.

5. My mum enjoys music she plays the harp beautifully.

6. It is raining outside consequently I must wear my coat.

7. I used many pizza toppings cheese, ham, mushrooms, and sweetcorn.

8. Russians like to play the following football, ice hockey, tennis and skiing.

9. Peter Fabergé was a famous jeweller he designed many beautiful eggs.

F Extension Ideas

Use the library or internet to help you with the following exercise.
Write two interesting facts about Fabergé eggs.

(a)

(b)

G **Writing Genre: Explanation Writing**

The Inuit people have lived in the tundra for over 1,000 years, a place where the climate is so severe that even trees and many animals are unable to survive.

Write an explanation on how the Inuit people have survived in the harsh climate of the tundra. Complete the template below.

Title: **How the Inuit Tribe Survive the Harsh Climate of the Tundra**

Definition (Who are the Inuit people?): _____

_____

How does it happen? _____

_____

Where does it happen? _____

When does it happen? _____

Why does it happen? _____

Interesting fact 1: _____

_____

Interesting fact 2: _____

_____

Now, write your explanation.

Title: **How the Inuit Tribe Survive the Harsh Climate of the Tundra**

_____

_____

_____

_____

_____

_____

_____

_____

_____

H **Self Reflection**

I was good at: _____

I need to do more work on: _____ Date: _____

A **A Little Light Thinking**

1. What colour was the car? _____

2. Why was Harry shocked to see Ron? _____

3. How many times had Ron asked Harry to stay?_____

4. Who does Ron's dad work for? _____

5. What did they tie around the bars in order to pull them?

   _____

6. Who drove the car? _____

7. What did Fred and George use to pick the lock on the door? _____

8. Who began to cough in another room? _____

9. What made the sudden loud screech? _____

10. What sentence tells us that Harry collected his things very quickly from his room?

    _____

B **Deeper Thinking**

1. Who do you think the Muggles are?

   _____

   _____

2. Why do you think they were not allowed to do spells outside of school?

   _____

   _____

3. How do we know that Hedwig realised how important it was to free Harry?

   _____

   _____

4. Why do you think Harry's Hogwarts stuff was locked under the stairs?

   _____

   _____

5. How do we know that Uncle Vernon was angry?

   _____

   _____

6. Why do you think George whispered, *OK, let's go*?

   _____

   _____

CHALLENGE

What do you think will happen to Harry when he returns to sceool?

_____

_____

C Vocabulary Work: Analogies

An **analogy** is a phrase used to show a resemblance or similarity in some way between two things that are otherwise not similar at all, e.g. **uncle** is to **nephew** as **aunt** is to **niece**.

Complete the following sentences using the most appropriate analogy in each case.

1. Boy is to girl as _____ is to woman.
2. Cat is to kitten as _____ is to pup.
3. Aunt is to woman as _____ is to man.
4. Nose is to smell as _____ is to taste.
5. Day is to week as _____ is to year.
6. Walk is to legs as _____ is to wings.
7. Artist is to _____ as author is to book.
8. Tear is to sorrow as smile is to _____.
9. High is to low as _____ is to down.
10. Sheep is to mutton as pig is to _____.
11. Wrist is to arm as ankle is to _____.
12. Here is to there as this is to _____.
13. Hearing is to ear as _____ is to eye.
14. Food is to hungry as _____ is to thirsty.
15. April is to May as _____ is to September.

D Working with Sounds: The Long /e/ Sound

The **long /e/** sound generally occurs:
(a) When /ea/ or /ee/ come together, e.g. m**ea**t / f**ee**t.
(b) When /y/ sounds like a vowel (**e**) at the end of a word, e.g. Harr**y** / obviousl**y**.
(c) When the vowel is at the end of a syllable (it is not closed by a consonant)
e.g. **e**ven (initial sound); imm**e**diately (medial sound); w**e** / m**e** (final sound).

Put the long /e/ words from the word box in the correct sentences below.

baby	family	legal	female
eclipse	sweets	seats	We

1. Ron was jerking his head towards the front _____ and grinning broadly.
2. A _____ horse is called a mare.
3. We waited up to watch the _____ of the sun and the moon.
4. The _____ wailed and rattled the cradle because it was hungry.
5. _____ entered the restaurant and ordered our starters straight away.
6. The _____ speed limit on motorways in Ireland is 120 km/h.
7. I live with my _____ in a two-storey house in the countryside.
8. I bought some _____ for my friend in the supermarket.

E Grammar: Adjectives

An **adjective** is a describing word. It tells us more about a noun, e.g.
The boys were travelling in an **old**, **turquoise** car in the **blue**, **cloudless** sky.

1. Write the adjective(s) from the story to complete the following sentences.

crunching	old, turquoise	elder, twin	dark	Uncle Vernon's
official	back	ruddy	floating	ordinary

(a) Fred and George were Ron's _____, _____ brothers.

(b) Ron was leaning out of the back window of an _____, _____ car.

(c) Dad said you got an _____ warning for using magic in front of Muggles.

(d) Harry told Ron it was a bit rich coming from him as he stared at the _____ car.

(e) With a _____ noise, the bars were pulled clean out of the window.

(f) George took an _____ hairpin from his pocket.

(g) The twins disappeared onto the _____ landing of the Dursley's house.

(h) The trunk slid out the window and into the _____ seat of the car.

(i) They could hear the sudden thunder of _____ _____ voice.

(j) Uncle Vernon screamed about the _____ owl.

2. Put the following adjectives in short sentences of your own.

(a) brave: _____

(b) calm: _____

(c) loyal: _____

(d) loud: _____

(e) front: _____

(f) silent: _____

(g) long: _____

(h) still: _____

F Extension Ideas

Use the library or internet to help you with the following exercise.

1. Name six models of car and the company that makes them.

(a) _____ (b) _____

(c) _____ (d) _____

(e) _____ (f) _____

2. Write four interesting facts about one of the cars you have named above.

(a) _____

(b) _____

(c) _____

(d) _____

G **Writing Genre: Explanation Writing**

In the story, we read about Ron in a flying car. There are many things that can fly, from birds to aeroplanes. Plan and write an explanation on how to fly a kite.

Title: **How to Fly a Kite**

Definition (What is a kite?): _____

What does it look like? _____

Where could you fly it? _____

How does it happen? _____

Why does it happen? _____

What is it used for? _____

Are there any interesting facts about kites? _____

_____

Special features: What do you need to be careful of when flying a kite?

_____

_____

Now, write your explanation.

Title: **How to Fly a Kite**

_____

_____

_____

_____

_____

_____

_____

_____

H Self Reflection

I was good at: _____

I need to do more work on: _____ Date: _____

A A Little Light Thinking

1. Where did Genzo find the little girl? _____

2. What precious stones did Genzo find in the stems of the bamboo he cut down?
   _____

3. Where was Mount Horai? _____

4. In what part of his body did the dragon carry the precious stone?
   _____

5. How long did it take the jewellers to make the golden branch? _____

6. In what did the second knight bring his precious gift back? _____

7. How did the princess know that the branch wasn't from Mount Horai?
   _____

8. What happened to the skin of the fire-rat when the princess dropped it in the fire?
   _____

B Deeper Thinking

1. How do you think Genzo felt when he found the princess in the bamboo? Explain.
   _____
   _____

2. How do you think the couple felt about keeping the princess as their child? Explain.
   _____
   _____

3. How do we know that the princess was very popular?
   _____
   _____

4. Why do you think the three suitors devised their schemes to make the princess think they had succeeded? _____
   _____

5. Why do you think each knight had to pay a huge amount of gold for their gifts?
   _____
   _____

6. Why do you think the couple called the girl *Princess Moonlight*?
   _____
   _____

CHALLENGE

What sentence tells us that the task given to the second knight was an **exceedingly dangerous one?**

_____
_____

An **anagram** is formed by rearranging **all** of the letters of a word to produce a new word, e.g. shoot → hoots / there → three / heart → earth / paces → space / later → alert.

1. Use the clues to write **anagrams** for the following words from the story.

(a)	sent	Used to catch fish	_____
(b)	could	White and fluffy in the sky	_____
(c)	was	Used for cutting wood	_____
(d)	lumps	Sit, lean or fall heavily	_____
(e)	mean	Long, thick hair on a horse's neck	_____
(f)	stone	Short letters or messages	_____
(g)	garden	A male goose	_____
(h)	brief	A thread or a small piece of material	_____
(i)	heat	To deeply dislike someone or something	_____
(j)	low	A nocturnal bird	_____

2. Write the clues to change the following anagrams.

(a)	slope	_____	poles
(b)	best	_____	bets
(c)	used	_____	sued
(d)	skill	_____	kills
(e)	death	_____	hated
(f)	cause	_____	sauce
(g)	silent	_____	listen
(h)	rage	_____	gear

D Working with Sounds: The Long /u/ Sound

The **long /u/** sound is pronounced as in words such as **you**. It occurs in the following:
(a) Sometimes when the letter **u** is the first syllable of a word, e.g. h**u**man.
(b) The magic **e** at the end of a word, e.g. p**u**re, c**u**te, t**u**be, c**u**be.
(c) When the letters **ew** come at the end of a word, e.g. gr**ew**, st**ew**, fl**ew**.

Write the following words with the long /u/ sound under the correct heading.

chew	immune	refuse	nephew	human	consume
produce	music	ruby	screw	uniform	duty
dune	future	mule	threw	knew	unit
huge	new	drew	cupid	student	flew

Long /u/ in first syllable		u with the magic e		Words ending in ew	
1. _____	2. _____	1. _____	2. _____	1. _____	2. _____
3. _____	4. _____	3. _____	4. _____	3. _____	4. _____
5. _____	6. _____	5. _____	6. _____	5. _____	6. _____
7. _____	8. _____	7. _____	8. _____	7. _____	8. _____

E **Grammar: Compound Words**

Compound words are formed when two smaller words are joined to make a new, bigger word, e.g. out + side → outside / foot + path → footpath.

1. **Match the words below to make compound words.**

earth ●	● fighter
fire ●	● fly
sun ●	● board
grand ●	● man
grass ●	● quake
butter ●	● flower
skate ●	● bone
pepper ●	● hopper
back ●	● mint
weather ●	● mother

basket ●	● corn
moon ●	● hero
life ●	● book
eye ●	● ball
text ●	● light
up ●	● bathe
under ●	● stairs
pop ●	● sight
super ●	● time
sun ●	● ground

2. **Make your own compound words below with the word given. Write it.**

day →	break	daybreak

(a)	up	_____	_____
(c)	water	_____	_____
(e)	black	_____	_____
(g)	car	_____	_____
(i)	grand	_____	_____

(b)	fire	_____	_____
(d)	tea	_____	_____
(f)	egg	_____	_____
(h)	dish	_____	_____
(j)	river	_____	_____

F **Extension Ideas**

Use the library or internet to help you with the following exercise.

1. **Name six products for which Japan is famous.**

   (a) _____ (b) _____ (c) _____

   (d) _____ (e) _____ (f) _____

2. **Write the names of six major companies originating in Japan.**

   (a) _____ (b) _____ (c) _____

   (d) _____ (e) _____ (f) _____

3. **If you could have any magical power:**

   (a) What would it be? _____

   (b) How would it be useful? _____

   (c) What would you do? _____

G Writing Genre: Writing to Socialise

Imagine you are the first knight sent to Mount Horai to get a branch from the wonderful tree. Write a letter to a friend telling them about your journey. Complete the template below.

Address: _____

_____

_____

Date: _____

Greeting: _____

Paragraph 1: _____

_____

_____

Paragraph 2: _____

_____

_____

Paragraph 3: _____

_____

_____

Farewell: _____

Sign off: _____

Now, write your letter.

Mount Horai,
Eastern Sea

August 542 AD

Dear _____,

_____

_____

H Self Reflection

I was good at: _____

I need to do more work on: _____ Date: _____

27 Japan

A A Little Light Thinking

1. What is the Japanese word for Japan? _____

2. In what ocean is Japan located? _____

3. What is the population of Japan? _____

4. What is the Pacific Ring of Fire? _____

5. What is the highest point in Japan? _____

6. Where did Japan bomb in December 1941? _____

7. Name three well-known brands developed in Japan.

   (a) _____ (b) _____ (c) _____

8. How many PlayStation 4 consoles did Sony sell worldwide? _____

9. What is the national sport of Japan? _____

10. When was (a) baseball introduced to Japan and (b) by whom?

    (a) _____ (b) _____

B Deeper Thinking

1. Why do you think Japan is referred to as *the land of the rising sun*?

   _____

   _____

2. Why do you think most people live in the cities?

   _____

   _____

3. Why do you think the land bridges connecting Japan to Russia and Korea are no longer there?

   _____

   _____

4. What reasons might Japan have for fighting against the USA during World War II?

   _____

   _____

5. Why do you think the Japanese are leaders in inventing new technology?

   _____

   _____

6. What makes Japanese cuisine healthier than most?

   _____

   _____

CHALLENGE

How do you think the Japanese could help teach other nations around the world?

_____

_____

C Vocabulary Work: Dictionary Meanings

Match the word from the story to its dictionary meaning below.

population	devastation	generation	contamination
emperor	banned	reigning	innovation

1. Great destruction or damage caused: _____

2. To be officially or legally prohibited: _____

3. All the people born or living around the same time: _____

4. Being made impure by polluting or poisoning: _____

5. The amount of people living in a certain country: _____

6. A new method, idea or product: _____

7. The sovereign ruler of an empire: _____

8. Occupying the throne or ruling as a sovereign: _____

D Comprehension Work: Cloze Procedure

Use the words in the word box to complete the story below.

forest	Pacific	tenth	emperor	islands
capital	radius	economies	overthrown	1868
failure	cities	China	common	evacuated
approximately	technology	archipelago	earthquakes	devastated

Japan

Japan is located in the _____ Ocean in Asia and lies off the coast of _____.
It is an island country. It is actually an _____ which is a collection of islands.
Japan consists of about 6,852 _____, in total.

Japan has the _____ largest population in the world at, _____,
127 million people. Over 90 percent of the population lives in _____ as three-quarters
of the land is either _____ or mountain. Tokyo is the _____ city of Japan.

Japan sits near the Pacific Ring of Fire which is an area where many _____ and
volcanoes occur. As a result, earthquakes are quite _____ in Japan. In 2011,
a strong earthquake hit Japan and killed nearly 22,000 people. It also caused a cooling
_____ at a nuclear plant in Fukushima. People from a 20 km _____ of the
plant had to be _____ in case they got exposed to radiation.

Japan is now the only country in the world to be ruled by an _____. Europeans
ruled Japan for more than 200 years until _____. The Europeans were _____
and the emperors returned to their rightful place.

In December 1941, Japan bombed Pearl Harbour in Hawaii causing the USA to enter World War II
on the opposite side to Japan. World War II _____ Japan's economy. However,
through hard work and superb innovation, Japan turned things around, now making it one
of the largest _____ in the world. Japan produces some of the world's leading
electronics brands including Canon, Sharp, Sony and Nintendo. Japanese innovation in the
_____ world has made it one of the top economies in the world.

E Word Sort: Classification

Every object can be placed in a general classification either because of resemblance or because of its purpose or use, e.g. Sharp, Nintendo and Sony → electronic brands.

Write the word in brackets that belongs with the group.

1. abandon, depart, leave (evacuate / allow / permit / remain) _____

2. collapse, decline, defeat (success / accomplishment / failure) _____

3. permitted, approved, authorised (disallowed / refused / allowed) _____

4. outlawed, prohibited, disallowed (banned / approved / sanctioned) _____

5. partner, colleague, friend (enemy / ally / foe / opponent) _____

6. compile, construct, produce (destroy / break / assemble / separate) _____

7. abundant, plentiful, ample (scarce / meagre / lacking / copious) _____

8. appreciation, regard, reverence (criticism / disdain / respect) _____

9. well-known, famous, prominent (unknown / popular / obscure) _____

10. accomplishment, achievement, victory (success / defeat / failure) _____

F Grammar: Abstract Nouns

An abstract noun is one you cannot see, feel, hear, touch or taste. It usually conveys an emotion or idea, e.g. sadness, happiness, sorrow, failure, love, death, truth, etc.

Match the following abstract nouns to their dictionary meanings below.

knowledge	friendship	misery	charity	awe
deceit	peace	justice	loyalty	liberty

1. A relationship between friends: _____

2. A time or period when there is no war: _____

3. A feeling of great physical or mental distress or discomfort: _____

4. Concealing or misrepresenting the truth: _____

5. A feeling of respect mixed with wonder or fear: _____

6. The voluntary giving of help, typically in the form of money: _____

7. Fair or just behaviour: _____

8. A strong feeling of support or allegiance: _____

9. Information and skills acquired through experience or education: _____

10. The state of being free from oppression: _____

G Extension Ideas

Use the library or internet to help you with the following exercise.

Write the names of six major brands produced in Japan.

(a) _____ (b) _____

(c) _____ (d) _____

(e) _____ (f) _____

H **Writing Genre: Writing to Socialise**

Imagine you won a competition to help Sony create a new game for the PlayStation 4.

Plan and write an email to your friend telling them about your experience in Japan, including what you have seen, your work with Sony and when you are returning home. Complete the template below.

To (email address): _____

Subject: _____

Greeting: _____

Paragraph 1: _____

_____

_____

_____

_____

Paragraph 2: _____

_____

_____

_____

_____

Paragraph 3: _____

_____

_____

_____

Farewell: _____

Sign off: _____

Now, write your email on page 136.

135

To: _____

Subject: _____

From: _____

Date: _____

Hi _____

_____

_____

_____

_____

_____

_____

_____

_____

_____

_____

_____

_____

_____

_____

_____

_____

Send   🗑 ▼

❶ Self Reflection

I was good at: _____

I need to do more work on: _____ Date: _____

The Wonderling 28

A A Little Light Thinking

1. What was painted on the Wonderling's hard, narrow bed?

   _____

2. What did his one ear look like? _____

3. Where did he keep his scrap of baby blanket? _____

4. What was wrapped inside the blanket? _____

5. What was the only thing he could remember from long ago?

   _____

6. What was the name of the orphanage?_____

7. Where was the only place they saw greenery in the orphanage?

   _____

8. What two types of creature were seen as one entered the orphanage?

   (a) _____   (b) _____

9. How many storeys high was the orphanage?_____

10. From what were the walls built centuries ago? _____

B Deeper Thinking

1. Why do you think he hated the name Number Thirteen so much?

   _____

2. What was unusual about his appearance?

   _____

3. What do you think happened to his ear?

   _____

4. What sentence tells us that he still needs to be comforted like a child?

   _____

   _____

5. What sentence tells us that the building had a strange, eerie past?

   _____

   _____

6. What type of person do you think Miss Carbunkle is? Explain.

   _____

   _____

CHALLENGE

Explain why you think more entered the orphanage than left it?

_____

137

C Vocabulary Work: Find the Word

1. Write six words from the story that include the smaller words in the top row of the grid. An example is given for each.

	and	the	red	ear	had	far
	comm**and**	toge**the**r	sh**red**ding	b**ear**ly	s**had**ing	**far**ther
(a)						
(b)						
(c)						
(d)						
(e)						
(f)						

2. What smaller word can you find in each of the following words?

(a) disliked: _____ (b) solace: _____ (c) unclaimed: _____ (d) recently: _____

(e) paper: _____ (f) fragment: _____ (g) innocent: _____ (h) misbegotten: _____

(i) heard: _____ (j) medieval: _____ (k) ordinary: _____ (l) surrounded: _____

(m) rabbit: _____ (n) entrance: _____ (o) burdened: _____ (p) dislodged: _____

(q) spear: _____ (r) responded: _____ (s) dangled: _____ (t) storeys: _____

D Working with Sounds: Suffix -ture

The **suffix -ture** at the end of a word sounds like /cher/, e.g. crea**ture**, frac**ture**, etc.

Ring 10 words with the -ture **suffix in the wordsearch.**

p	m	v	x	m	e	r	u	t	a	e	f
w	e	r	u	t	u	f	e	j	a	w	k
x	b	e	n	t	t	r	t	z	g	f	s
e	t	d	v	a	d	o	j	g	r	i	s
r	e	j	e	p	t	w	z	s	i	x	t
u	r	d	y	p	t	u	w	e	c	t	a
t	u	t	h	q	a	v	r	o	u	u	t
c	t	j	c	d	m	r	o	e	l	r	u
i	a	b	l	a	r	f	t	s	t	e	r
p	e	r	u	t	p	a	c	u	u	g	e
w	r	y	w	q	d	v	b	x	r	i	a
s	c	d	r	w	p	k	k	k	e	e	o

creature ↑   departure ↘

agriculture ↓   capture ←

stature ↓   future ←

nature ↘   feature ←

picture ↑   fixture ↓

E **Grammar: Contractions**

A contraction is a shortened version of a word using an apostrophe to replace the missing letter(s) e.g. he'd → he would / couldn't → could not / let's → let us / she's → she is.

Rewrite the following sentences using a contraction for the underlined words.

1. 'Did you know that <u>he is</u> one of my best friends?' she asked.

   _____

2. '<u>They will</u> show us around the museum when we arrive,' he explained.

   _____

3. 'I think <u>it will</u> be very interesting to see how she deals with the situation,' I said.

   _____

4. 'I know <u>he will</u> arrive on time because <u>he is</u> never late for anything,' Mum said.

   _____

5. '<u>We will</u> do very well in the soccer tournament as we have a great team,' they said.

   _____

6. 'I <u>would not</u> be surprised if she <u>did not</u> bring the parcel to the party,' said Sandra.

   _____

7. 'I think <u>she will</u> come first in the race and <u>he will</u> finish second,' she said.

   _____

8. '<u>You will</u> have to go to the market early or <u>there will</u> be no fruit left,' I said.

   _____

9. 'You <u>should not</u> go outside unless <u>you have</u> put on your jacket,' she said.

   _____

10. '<u>I have</u> the flu so I think <u>I will</u> stay in bed for another hour,' said Amelia.

    _____

11. 'I <u>could not</u> believe that she <u>has not</u> changed since I met her last,' said Tara.

    _____

12. '<u>She will</u> not be over until <u>you are</u> on the way to the game,' said Mum.

    _____

F **Extension Ideas**

Use the library or internet to help you with the following exercise.

Name six things that people think bring them bad luck.

(a) _____   (b) _____

(c) _____   (d) _____

(e) _____   (f) _____

G **Writing Genre: Narrative Writing**

Imagine if you were Number Thirteen and you have decided to escape from the orphanage. Plan and write your story titled: *The Day I Escaped from the Orphanage*. Complete the template.

Title: **The Day I Escaped from the Orphanage**

Who is the story about? _____

Where does the story take place? _____

When did the story happen? _____

How did the characters get involved? _____

_____

What is the conflict/problem? _____

_____

Resolution: How was the problem resolved? _____

_____

Now, write your story.

Title: **The Day I Escaped from the Orphanage**

_____

_____

_____

_____

_____

_____

_____

_____

_____

_____

_____

H **Self Reflection**

I was good at: _____

I need to do more work on: _____ Date: _____

29 Driving Through Africa

A A Little Light Thinking

1. For how long had the war been going on when Roald Dahl told the Shell Company he was leaving? _____

2. How far was it from Dar es Salaam to Nairobi? _____

3. What trees did the giraffes feed on? _____

4. Describe the roads through the country of Tanganyika.

_____

5. How many men did it take to pull the raft across the river? _____

6. What were the only creatures that elephants had to fear in the wild?

_____

7. Where was the outpost of Customs and Immigration situated?

_____

8. Why was Roald not afraid while sleeping in the jungle?

_____

9. Why do you think Roald wanted to join the war effort? _____

10. In what city was the aerodrome situated? _____

B Deeper Thinking

1. In what month in 1939 did World War II begin? _____

2. What sentence tells us that the Shell Company was a good company to work for?

_____

_____

3. What sentence tells us that Roald had a great fear of snakes?

_____

4. How do we know that Roald was in awe of the elephant family?

_____

5. Why do you think the tribesmen were patting the car and looking at Roald, curiously?

_____

6. Why do you think it wasn't ideal for someone six feet six inches to fly an aeroplane?

_____

CHALLENGE

Why do you think there are passport control areas in airports and ports, at which travellers have to show their passports in order to enter the country?

_____

_____

C Vocabulary Work: Movement

While Roald Dahl travelled in Africa, he looked to the movement of the animals, e.g.
The snakes slithered over the boulders and through the deep undergrowth of the jungle.

Use the word box to describe the movement of the following creatures.

| galloped | leaped | swung | waddled | glided |
| prowled | lumbered | charged | scampered | walked |

1. The mouse _____ across the room with the piece of cheese.

2. The lion _____ through the jungle looking for its next prey.

3. The seagull _____ through the air and landed on top of the lighthouse.

4. The bear _____ clumsily from its cave and sat with a thud on the ground.

5. The monkey _____ from branch to branch in the jungle.

6. The horse _____ gracefully and quickly across the meadow.

7. The burglar _____ quietly out the door and disappeared down the street.

8. The frog _____ from lily pad to lily pad on the pond.

9. The duck _____ slowly towards the piece of bread on the ground.

10. The bull _____ angrily across the field when it spotted the dog.

D Working With Sounds: Suffixes **-ous** and **-ious**

The suffixes **-ous** and **-ious** mean *full of* and usually have an /us/ sound, e.g. hazard**ous**, humor**ous**, infam**ous**, mali**cious**, cons**cious**, deli**cious**, subcons**cious**, fero**cious**, etc.
In words ending in **-ious**, the **i** often has a /y/ sound e.g. cur**ious**, ser**ious**, ted**ious**, etc.

Ring the 10 -ous and -ious words in the wordsearch.

e	y	n	f	h	l	m	x	h	e	d	k
n	o	j	a	t	b	p	e	s	d	i	a
o	t	u	b	s	k	r	g	n	s	e	c
r	x	m	u	q	s	e	d	u	v	a	u
m	o	a	l	u	q	v	o	w	z	n	r
o	j	l	o	a	s	i	o	f	a	x	i
u	h	m	u	e	c	o	z	e	f	i	o
s	a	s	s	i	i	u	y	l	o	o	u
f	m	v	l	l	n	s	u	p	n	u	s
r	g	e	n	e	r	o	u	s	n	s	f
t	d	i	s	a	s	t	r	o	u	s	u
y	m	f	w	n	e	r	v	o	u	s	k

disastrous →   generous →

fabulous ↓   curious ↓

enormous ↓   nervous →

anxious ↓   previous ↓

delicious ↗   famous ↗

E Grammar: Possessive Pronouns

Possessive pronouns are used to show possession or ownership in a sentence.
The possessive pronouns are: mine, yours, his, hers, ours, its, theirs.
Be careful not to mix up possessive pronouns with **possessive adjectives**!

1. Write the possessive pronouns in each of the following.

   (a) I didn't have a book, so Dan gave me his.   (i) _____

   (b) 'Now that you have a pen, can I have mine back?' she asked. (i) _____

   (c) 'That ball is ours,' said the children to the old lady.   (i) _____

   (d) 'That coat is hers and definitely not his,' said Paula.   (i) _____ (ii) _____

   (e) 'That hat of yours is similar to mine,' said Aoife.   (i) _____ (ii) _____

   (f) 'Are any of these books his or are any hers?' asked Dad.   (i) _____ (ii) _____

   (g) 'These apples are ours, not theirs,' said Tim.   (i) _____ (ii) _____

   (h) Hers is in the wash, so may I use yours?' asked Mal.   (i) _____ (ii) _____

   (i) Mine was broken, so I decided to use his instead.   (i) _____ (ii) _____

   (j) Ours is a fine shed but theirs is an absolute wreck.   (i) _____ (ii) _____

2. Complete the following sentences with the most suitable possessive pronoun.

   (a) 'This is Katy's pen on the table. Is this one _____, Danny?' asked Aisling.

   (b) 'Those books are _____,' said the children to the librarian.

   (c) 'Dad liked his present but Mum didn't like _____,' said Sarah.

   (d) 'Michelle thought the toy was hers but it was actually _____,' said Niamh.

   (e) 'These are our books but those are _____,' said the children.

   (f) 'This is _____ and that is _____,' said Simona to Sofia.

   (g) 'We are going to get what is rightly _____ in the will,' said Eoin and Orla.

   (h) 'The dress is _____ but the trousers are _____,' said Mum to Clara and Cian.

   (i) 'The red bibs are ours but the blue bibs are _____,' said the captain.

   (j) 'That bar in not _____! It is _____!' cried Jane angrily.

F Extension Ideas

Use the library or internet to help you with the following exercise.

1. Write the names of six animals found in the wild in Africa.

   (a) _____   (b) _____

   (c) _____   (d) _____

   (e) _____   (f) _____

2. Write five interesting facts about giraffes.

   (a) _____

   (b) _____

   (c) _____

   (d) _____

   (e) _____

G **Writing Genre: Narrative Writing**

Roald Dahl spent two days driving through Central Africa on his own. He encountered many strange and terrifying incidents along the way. Imagine you are on a jungle trek through Africa. Write a narrative story titled: *My Trip Through Africa*.
Complete the template below.

Title: **My Trip Through Africa**

Where does the story take place? _____

When does the story happen? _____

What is the weather or climate like? _____

What can you see? _____

What can you smell? _____

What can you hear? _____

What can you touch? _____

What can you taste? _____

What is the landscape like? _____

How does this place make you feel? _____

Now, write your story.

Title: **My Trip Through Africa**

_____

_____

_____

_____

_____

_____

_____

_____

_____

_____

_____

_____

H Self Reflection

I was good at: _____

I need to do more work on: _____ Date: _____

A A Little Light Thinking

1. How is the male African lion easily identifiable? _____

2. What is the usual habitat of the African lion? _____

3. What is the name given to a group of lions? _____

4. How many lion cubs are there usually in a litter? _____

5. To what length does an Amur tiger grow? _____

6. For how long do tigers usually live? _____

7. What does the word *jaguar* mean?_____

8. Leopards are nocturnal animals. What is the meaning of the word *nocturnal*?

   _____

B Deeper Thinking

1. Why do you think most of these big cats are endangered species today?

   _____

   _____

2. Why do you think lions will only attack rhinos, hippos and elephants, if food is scarce?

   _____

   _____

3. Why do you think it is important for the tiger that its coat acts as camouflage?

   _____

   _____

4. What makes jaguars different to most other big cats?

   _____

   _____

5. Give two reasons why you know that the jaguar is a very powerful creature.

   (a) _____

   (b) _____

6. What sentence tells us that the leopard is a very strong animal?

   _____

   _____

CHALLENGE

Why do you think leopards are rarely seen by humans?

_____

_____

C Vocabulary Work: True or False?

Write true or false after these statements.

1. The African lion is a small animal. _____

2. Lions are herbivores, eating only plants. _____

3. A lion's roar can be heard as far as 8 km away. _____

4. The tiger weighs approximately the same as five humans. _____

5. The Caspian tiger is the most common tiger in the world. _____

6. Jaguars are afraid of the water. _____

7. There are thousands of jaguars living in the USA. _____

8. The leopard is the smallest of the big cats. _____

9. Leopards hunt during the day. _____

10. Leopards can live for up to 18 years in the wild. _____

D Comprehension Work: Cloze Procedure

Use the words in the word box to complete the story below.

species	eliminated	leopard	group	metres	largest	rainforests
fangs	Asia	male	Amazon	mane	extinct	nocturnal
plants	prey	powerful	scavengers	impressive	carnivores	massive

Big Cats

The lion, the tiger, the jaguar and the leopard are among the world's most _____ and powerful animals and almost all of them are in the endangered _____ category.

The African lion is a _____ animal. The adult _____ is easy to recognise by the _____ of hair around its head and neck. This begins to grow when the male cub is about 10 months old. Lions are _____, relying on meat rather than _____ for food. They live in a family _____ called a pride.

The tiger is the _____ of all the cats. It can grow to over 3 _____ in length and can weigh up to 350 kg. It has the largest and sharpest _____ of any big cat. It is found in a small area of _____. Many of the tiger sub-species have become _____.

The jaguar lives in the jungles, _____ and swamps of South and Central America. Unlike most big cats, jaguars like the water and hunt crocodiles, anacondas, turtles and caiman from the _____ River. Jaguars were hunted for their fur and have been completely _____ from the USA.

The _____ is the smallest of the big cats but is probably the most _____ of them. It is incredibly strong and can carry _____ that is heavier than itself high up into the branches of a tree. It does this so that _____ can't steal its food. Leopards are _____ hunters and can run at speeds of up to 60 km/h.

E **Working with Words: Wordsearch**

Ring the following words in the wordsearch.

a	o	c	c	a	r	n	i	v	o	r	e
y	g	a	c	k	o	m	z	o	t	g	f
b	k	m	h	r	d	e	m	i	k	j	l
w	v	o	e	u	o	l	l	t	w	a	i
s	w	u	w	n	v	c	w	r	n	g	y
e	c	f	p	m	d	j	o	r	n	u	m
i	q	l	d	r	v	a	u	d	p	a	g
c	j	a	l	k	i	t	n	s	i	r	e
e	o	g	i	s	c	d	y	g	l	l	h
p	k	e	o	o	q	a	e	h	e	s	e
s	d	m	n	t	w	u	q	y	r	r	p
y	x	g	w	b	h	d	g	c	u	b	b

lion ↓   crocodile ↘

species ↑   nocturnal ↗

jaguar ↓   camouflage ↓

cub →   pride ↘

carnivore →   endanger ↘

F **Grammar: Alphabetical Order – Revision**

1. **Write these words from the extract in alphabetical order.**

   (a) species, stalking, social, solitary: _____ _____ _____ _____

   (b) prey, pride, prey, protect: _____ _____ _____ _____

   (c) central, cats, cub, crocodiles: _____ _____ _____ _____

   (d) lioness, lethal, leopard, leap: _____ _____ _____ _____

   (e) tiger, territorial, tropical, trees: _____ _____ _____ _____

   (f) adult, antelope, affect, appear: _____ _____ _____ _____

   (g) birds, buffalo, blind, brown: _____ _____ _____ _____

   (h) elephant, endanger, eat, effort: _____ _____ _____ _____

   (i) massive, mount, mothers, marsh: _____ _____ _____ _____

   (j) fend, food, family, first: _____ _____ _____ _____

2. **Write the correct spelling of these difficult words.**

   (a) acchieve / achieve _____   (b) millennium / millenium _____

   (c) acceptable / aceptable _____   (d) privilege / priviledge _____

   (e) abcense / absence _____   (f) potatos / potatoes _____

   (g) amature / amateur _____   (h) mispell / misspell _____

   (i) apparant / apparent _____   (j) wether / weather _____

   (k) adress / address _____   (l) wierd / weird _____

G **Extension Ideas**

Write the names of three more species of cat.

(a) _____   (b) _____   (c) _____

H Writing Genre: Free Writing

Write for 15 minutes describing what is happening in the following picture.
You can use words from the word box, if you need to. You can write in any genre you like.
Give your story a title.

prowling	silent	hunter	striped	canine teeth
growl	fierce	stalking	predator	carnivore
wild	paws	tail	whiskers	pounce

Now, write your piece in the genre of your choice.

Title: _____

_____

_____

_____

_____

_____

_____

_____

Self Reflection

I was good at: _____

I need to do more work on: _____ Date: _____

Notes

Notes

Notes